I0842554

Dr Peter Zupancic (b. 1946 in Oberhausen, Germany) is a retired English teacher and headmaster and author of several articles on castaway stories and didactic books on aspects of English literature. He is married and has three adult children.

Peter Zupancic

Would You Have Known?
A Quiz on Britain and the USA

Bibliografische Information der Deutschen Nationalbibliothek:
Die Deutsche Nationalbibliothek verzeichnet diese Publikation
in der Deutschen Nationalbibliografie; detaillierte bibliografische Daten sind im Internet über dnb.dnb.de abrufbar.

Herstellung und Verlag: BoD – Books on Demand, Norderstedt

Umschlaggestaltung und Satz: Philip Zupancic

Fotos: Julia, Marie-Christine und Philip Zupancic

ISBN: 978-3-748-15791-5

Dear Quizzer,

Welcome to a kaleidoscope of facts.

You are a businessman/businesswoman or tourist who visits GB and/or the USA regularly; a student, teacher or friend of English and the English-speaking world; or simply a native speaker of English.

The following 800 items will test your knowledge of British and American history, politics, geography, culture, literature, music, sport, customs, films, sights, eminent people etc. Do not hesitate to do the quiz together with expert friends if you feel you need help.

The quiz has two targets. On the one hand it is to show you how much you remember concerning the aforementioned fields of knowledge you once heard or read about or dealt with. On the other hand the quiz is going to provide you with a treasure chest of facts which are worth knowing and which will definitely enlarge and improve your general knowledge.

I wish you patience, pleasure and a lot of success.

Peter Zupancic

1 The famous Bayeux tapestry (70m long, 50cm wide) shows the Battle of
- ☐ Hastings (1066)
- ☐ Agincourt (1415)
- ☐ Crécy (1346).

2 Of the following three
- ☐ California
- ☐ Texas
- ☐ Montana

has the largest land area.

3 Which novel title is wrong?
- ☐ *Harry Potter and the Philosopher's Stone*
- ☐ *Harry Potter and the Deathly Hallows*
- ☐ *Harry Potter and the Prisoner of Azbakan*

4 'Gaol' rhymes with
- ☐ foal
- ☐ fail
- ☐ foul.

5 Elizabeth II became Queen of England in
- ☐ 1952
- ☐ 1972
- ☐ 1962.

6 In the USA Thanksgiving is celebrated on
- ☐ the second Sunday in November
- ☐ the fourth Sunday in October
- ☐ the fourth Thursday in November.

7 The change of the British currency to the present decimal system happened on
- ☐ 31 October 1968
- ☐ 1 June 1973
- ☐ 15 February 1971.

8 Which of these parks in London are closely together?
- ☐ Hyde Park and St James's Park
- ☐ Kensington Gardens and Hyde Park
- ☐ Regent's Park and Green Park

9   On the National Mall in Washington, D.C.
☐ the Washington Monument
☐ the Jefferson Memorial
☐ the White House
is between the Lincoln Memorial and the US Capitol.

10   *The Wind in the Willows* (1908), a children's novel,
was written by
☐ Beatrix Potter
☐ Kenneth Grahame
☐ Lewis Carroll.

11   'Pomp and Circumstance', a set of five marches, was
composed by
☐ Benjamin Britten
☐ Edward Elgar
☐ Sir William Walton.

12   In *Kind Hearts and Coronets* (1949), Sir Alec
Guinness played
☐ eight
☐ three
☐ five
parts, both male and female.

13   The Watergate Scandal (1974) was revealed by
reporters of
☐ the New York Times
☐ the International Herald Tribune
☐ the Washington Post.

14   The former British colony Rhodesia is now called
☐ Tanzania
☐ Botswana
☐ Zimbabwe.

15   The second astronaut to step on the moon was
☐ Neil Armstrong
☐ Buzz Aldrin
☐ Michael Collins.

16 Which spelling is correct?
- ☐ Sherlock Holmes
- ☐ Sherlok Holmes
- ☐ Sherlock Homes

17 'Ode to a Nightingale' is a long poem by
- ☐ John Keats
- ☐ William Wordsworth
- ☐ Samuel Taylor Coleridge.

18 Which of them suffered from stuttering?
- ☐ King George V
- ☐ King Edward VIII
- ☐ King George VI

19 Who was England never invaded by?
- ☐ Normans
- ☐ the Spanish
- ☐ Danish Vikings

20 The capital of Texas is
- ☐ Dallas
- ☐ Houston
- ☐ Austin.

21 The Bodleian Library is the main library of
- ☐ London University
- ☐ Cambridge University
- ☐ Oxford University.

22 Which of these Underground lines connects Heathrow Airport with the London city centre?
- ☐ the Piccadilly Line
- ☐ the District Line
- ☐ the Central Line

23 The Crown Jewels are in
- ☐ Buckingham Palace
- ☐ the British Museum
- ☐ the Tower of London.

A view of Manhattan, New York City.

In *Journal of the Plague Year* (1722) Daniel Defoe describes the great pestilence in

24
- ☐ Gloucester
- ☐ London
- ☐ Bristol.

The world's first railway in which passengers were carried on steam trains in the 1820s ran between

25
- ☐ Stockton and Darlington
- ☐ Newcastle and Sunderland
- ☐ Durham and Chester le Street.

Which of these cities has lost population most dramatically over the last 30 years?

26
- ☐ Detroit
- ☐ Baltimore
- ☐ Cleveland

Porgy and Bess (1935), a musical play, was composed by

27
- ☐ Cole Porter
- ☐ George Gershwin
- ☐ Oscar Hammerstein.

Anglo-Saxon is identical with

28
- ☐ Norman French
- ☐ Danish
- ☐ Old English.

29

Which statement is correct?
- ☐ Captain James Cook was killed on Tahiti.
- ☐ Cook conducted his expeditions in the first half of the 18th century.
- ☐ Cook learned his seamanship at Whitby.

30

The First Folio, the first collection of Shakespeare's plays, was published in
- ☐ 1623
- ☐ 1616
- ☐ 1630.

31

Which of these cities was called 'Eboracum' by the Romans?
- ☐ Bath
- ☐ York
- ☐ Chester

32

When London has 12 o'clock in the daytime San Diego in California has
- ☐ 8 p.m.
- ☐ 4 a.m.
- ☐ 5 a.m.

33

Hampton Court, a grand palace beside the River Thames, was built for
- ☐ King Henry VII
- ☐ King Edward VI
- ☐ King Henry VIII.

34

Diwali, the festival of lights, is celebrated in Britain every October or November by
- ☐ Indians
- ☐ Pakistanis
- ☐ people from the Caribbean.

35

Which of these former colonies was once called the Gold Coast?
- ☐ Nigeria
- ☐ Ghana
- ☐ Cameroon

36

The Concorde, the first passenger plane to fly faster than the speed of sound (London-New York in under three hours), was designed by
- ☐ the British
- ☐ the British and the French
- ☐ the Americans, the British and the French.

37

Silverstone, Britain's main motor racing track, is near
- ☐ Coventry
- ☐ Nottingham
- ☐ Northampton.

38

In his short life James Dean acted in
- ☐ three
- ☐ five
- ☐ four

movies.

39

In George Orwell's *Nineteen Eighty-Four* (1949) Winston Smith is afraid of
- ☐ Room 101
- ☐ Big Brother
- ☐ a new war between Eurasia and Oceania.

40

Which of the three statements is wrong?
- ☐ Robert the Bruce defeated the English at Bannockburn in 1314.
- ☐ Bonny Prince Charlie defeated the English at Culloden in 1746.
- ☐ William Wallace defeated the English at Stirling Bridge in 1297.

41

The highest mountain in the UK is
- ☐ Scafell Pike
- ☐ Mt Snowdon
- ☐ Ben Nevis.

In Robert Louis Stevenson's *Treasure Island* (1883)
Long John Silver, a pirate, has

42
- ☐ a parrot on his shoulder
- ☐ but one arm
- ☐ a fierce dog at his side.

One of the following is not a pet form of 'Elizabeth':

43
- ☐ Betsy
- ☐ Libby
- ☐ Ellie.

How often was Harold Wilson (Labour Party) elected Prime Minister?

44
- ☐ twice
- ☐ once
- ☐ three times

The national symbol of the United States is

45
- ☐ the lark
- ☐ the bald eagle
- ☐ the owl.

Hadrian's Wall was built as a protection against

46
- ☐ the Welsh
- ☐ the Scots
- ☐ the Irish.

The capital of Arizona is

47
- ☐ Phoenix
- ☐ Flagstaff
- ☐ Tucson.

The Barbican Centre in London is

48
- ☐ a large cultural centre
- ☐ a huge department store
- ☐ a famous flea market.

D.H. Lawrence wrote three versions of

49
- ☐ *Lady Chatterley's Lover*
- ☐ *Sons and Lovers*
- ☐ *Women in Love.*

Broadway Tower, Worcestershire, UK.

In 1895 the London Proms were started by

50
- ☐ Sir Thomas Beecham
- ☐ Sir William Walton
- ☐ Sir Henry Wood.

Cheers, a popular US comedy TV programme of the 1980s and 1990s, is set in

51
- ☐ New York
- ☐ Chicago
- ☐ Boston.

Without success Robert Devereux, second Earl of Essex, tried to turn the people of London against

52
- ☐ King James I
- ☐ Queen Mary I
- ☐ Queen Elizabeth I

and was beheaded.

One of the following counties is British but not English:

53
- ☐ Cumbria
- ☐ Antrim
- ☐ Dorset.

Pierre l'Enfant was

54
- ☐ a governer of Louisiana
- ☐ an architect who designed Washington, D.C.
- ☐ a mayor of New Orleans.

55

The English word 'regal' is of
- ☐ Latin
- ☐ Danish
- ☐ Old Saxon

origin.

56

The first editor of *The Oxford English Dictionary (OED)* was
- ☐ Sir James Murray
- ☐ Dr Samuel Johnson
- ☐ Noah Webster.

57

Who followed Winston Churchill as Prime Minister in 1945?
- ☐ Clement Attlee
- ☐ Sir Anthony Eden
- ☐ Harold Macmillan

58

The Magna Carta was signed by
- ☐ King John near London in 1215
- ☐ King John in York in 1215
- ☐ King Henry III near London in 1315.

59

The highest mountain in the USA is
- ☐ Mt Whitney
- ☐ Mt McKinley
- ☐ Mt Pikes Peak.

60

When someone is knighted by Queen Elizabeth II he has the title
- ☐ Sire
- ☐ Lord
- ☐ Sir.

61

The London stop for trains from the south of England is
- ☐ St Pancras Station
- ☐ Victoria Station
- ☐ Marylebone Station.

62 The United Nations Building in New York is in
☐ Midtown
☐ the Upper West Side
☐ the Lower East Side of Manhattan.

63 The quotation 'But to the girdle do the gods inherit,/Beneath is all the fiend's' is taken from Shakespeare's
☐ *Richard III*
☐ *Othello*
☐ *King Lear.*

64 When did Hawaii join the US as the 50th state?
☐ 1945
☐ 1952
☐ 1959

65 The
☐ Rio Grande
☐ Colorado River
☐ Missouri River
has cut a remarkable number of extremely deep trenches.

66 The composer George Frideric Handel lived in London from 1712 to 1759 and was a subject of
☐ King George I and King George II
☐ King George I
☐ King George II.

67 These are
☐ the womens
☐ the women's
☐ the womens'
bikes.

68 Penicillin was discovered by
☐ Dr Joseph Lister
☐ Sir Alexander Fleming
☐ Alexander Graham Bell.

69 In Defoe's *Robinson Crusoe* (1719) the hero is cast on an uninhabited island in
☐ the Caribbean Sea
☐ the Pacific Ocean
☐ the Indian Ocean.

70 The British Labour Party was formed in
☐ 1919
☐ 1890
☐ 1906.

71 The largest city of New Zealand is
☐ Christchurch
☐ Wellington
☐ Auckland.

72 Queen Victoria reigned
☐ from 1840 to 1899
☐ from 1837 to 1901
☐ from 1845 to 1903.

73 'Speakeasies' were places in the USA in the 1920s and 1930s where
☐ you could buy alcohol illegally.
☐ you could meet US special agents secretly.
☐ you could publicly criticize the US government.

74 'Though' rhymes with
☐ dough
☐ rough
☐ enough.

75 The Kennedy Space Center is in
☐ Texas
☐ New Mexico
☐ Florida.

76 Which football team plays in a stadium called 'Old Trafford' and 'Theatre of Dreams'?
☐ FC Chelsea
☐ Manchester United
☐ Tottenham Hotspur

The iconic Hollywood Sign on the Hollywood Hills, Los Angeles.

77 Gatwick International Airport is
☐ north
☐ west
☐ south
of London.

78 In the British TV comedy series
☐ Yes, Minister
☐ Fawlty Towers
☐ Spitting Image
large rubber models were used to make fun of famous people by making them do and say ridiculous things.

79 William Frederick Cody was also called
☐ Buffalo Bill
☐ Doc Holliday
☐ Billy the Kid.

80 The British passenger ship Titanic sank in
☐ mid-April 1914
☐ mid-November 1912
☐ mid-April 1912.

81 The biggest city in Scotland is
☐ Edinburgh
☐ Glasgow
☐ Aberdeen.

82 Excalibur is the name of a magic
- ☐ sword
- ☐ castle
- ☐ island.

83 Which spelling is correct?
- ☐ Caribbean
- ☐ Carribean
- ☐ Caribean

84 Queen Victoria was also Empress of
- ☐ Australia
- ☐ India
- ☐ New Zealand.

85 Which statement is correct? The Commonwealth Games take place
- ☐ in London
- ☐ in different former colonies every five years
- ☐ every four years.

86 The capital of Maryland (US) is
- ☐ Hagerstown
- ☐ Baltimore
- ☐ Annapolis.

87 Central Park in NYC has the form of a/an
- ☐ rectangle
- ☐ oval
- ☐ square.

88 The British Museum in London is in
- ☐ Marylebone W 1
- ☐ Bloomsbury WC 1
- ☐ Holborn WC 2.

89 Who wrote the famous *Tarzan* stories?
- ☐ William Burroughs
- ☐ Edgar Rice Burroughs
- ☐ Anthony Burgess

The New York Philharmonic regularly performs in

90
- ☐ the Carnegie Hall
- ☐ the Madison Square Garden
- ☐ the Avery Fisher Hall.

In motion pictures, a process in which three synchronized movie projectors each project one third of the picture on a wide and curving screen is called

91
- ☐ Cinerama
- ☐ CinemaScope
- ☐ Panavision.

The Act of Supremacy (1534) meant that

92
- ☐ King Henry VIII was finally allowed to divorce Catharine of Aragon, his first wife.
- ☐ King Henry VIII was made the head of the Church of England.
- ☐ England proclaimed itself the leading naval power of Europe.

Manchester is between

93
- ☐ Birmingham and Liverpool
- ☐ Liverpool and Leeds
- ☐ Nottingham and Sheffield.

Sir Samuel Cunard (1787 – 1865) founded

94
- ☐ the British Museum in London
- ☐ Warwick University
- ☐ the first regular Atlantic steamship line.

95
- ☐ Fudge
- ☐ Nudge
- ☐ Budge

is a soft creamy brown sweet food.

The action in Shakespeare's *Romeo and Juliet* is set in

96
- ☐ Verona
- ☐ Venice
- ☐ Valencia.

97

In 1998 US President Bill Clinton became the
- ☐ first
- ☐ second
- ☐ third

president to be impeached.

98

In 1485 King Richard III was killed in the Battle of
- ☐ Flodden
- ☐ Agincourt
- ☐ Bosworth Field.

99

Which is the capital of Florida?
- ☐ Tallahassee
- ☐ Fort Myers
- ☐ Jacksonville

100

The national saint of England is
- ☐ St Patrick
- ☐ St George
- ☐ St Andrew.

101

- ☐ Logan Airport
- ☐ O'Hare Airport
- ☐ Dulles Airport

is the international airport of Chicago.

102

Whose head made of rock cannot be seen on Mount Rushmore in South Dakota?
- ☐ Thomas Jefferson
- ☐ Ulysses S. Grant
- ☐ Theodore Roosevelt

103

The *Encyclopedia Britannica* was first published in 1768 in
- ☐ Chicago
- ☐ London
- ☐ Edinburgh.

The seaside town of Whitby in North Yorkshire, England.

104 The American Declaration of Independence took place on
- ☐ 4 July 1776
- ☐ 14 July 1776
- ☐ 4 July 1789.

105 Which of the following pairs of cities has roughly the same number of inhabitants?
- ☐ Bristol and Brighton
- ☐ Cardiff and Coventry
- ☐ Leicester and Luton

106 Which of these are the initials of a famous American orchestra?
- ☐ RPO
- ☐ CSO
- ☐ LSO

107 Which plural form is wrong?
- ☐ criterias
- ☐ crises
- ☐ appendixes

108 Paul Neal 'Red' Adair (1915 – 2004) was
- ☐ a Texan oil well firefighter
- ☐ a senator for Texas
- ☐ a US army general from Texas.

109

As the future King of England Prince Charles would be
☐ King Charles III
☐ King Charles II
☐ King Charles IV.

110

England was not a monarchy but a republic between
☐ 1702 and 1714
☐ 1603 and 1611
☐ 1649 and 1660.

111

Barack Obama was the
☐ 40th
☐ 42nd
☐ 44th
President of the United States.

112

Roman administration in England ended at about
☐ the end of the 2nd century A.D.
☐ the beginning of the 5th century A.D.
☐ the middle of the 3rd century A.D.

113

The capital of New York State is
☐ Albany
☐ New York City
☐ Rochester.

114

Little Dorrit (1855f.) was written by
☐ Charles Dickens
☐ William Makepeace Thackeray
☐ George Eliot.

115

The phrase 'in the nick of time' means
☐ just before it is too late
☐ step by step
☐ not too fast.

116

☐ The Wrigley Building
☐ The Playboy Building
☐ The Time Warner Center
is not in Chicago.

117

Which statement is wrong?   The British Prime Minister
☐ has regular meetings with the sovereign.
☐ is First Lord of the Treasury.
☐ is head of state.

118

In 2013 archaeologists found the skeleton of
☐ Oliver Cromwell
☐ King Richard III
☐ King Henry VII
under a car park in Leicester.

119

In the 19th century the USA
☐ conquered Alaska easily.
☐ bought Alaska from Russia.
☐ bought Alaska from France.

120

The United Kingdom is
☐ Britain and Ulster
☐ England, Scotland and Wales
☐ Britain and the Republic of Ireland.

121

'Samuel Langhorne Clemens' was the real name of
☐ Henry James
☐ Mark Twain
☐ Nathaniel Hawthorne.

122

'The Young Person's Guide to the Orchestra' was composed by
☐ Benjamin Britten
☐ Elliott Carter
☐ Leonard Bernstein.

123

The first *Jurassic Park*-movie directed by Steven Spielberg was released in
☐ 1985
☐ 1993
☐ 1999.

124 The four Dalton Brothers
☐ were train and bank robbers in the USA.
☐ were famous US singers of country music.
☐ founded a film company in Hollywood in the 1930s.

125 ☐ LaGuardia Airport
☐ J.F.K. International Airport
☐ Newark International Airport
is closest to Manhattan.

126 Which statement is wrong? In the British succession to the throne,
☐ the House of Hanover was followed by the Stuarts.
☐ the Houses of Lancaster and York were followed by the Tudors.
☐ the House of Saxe-Coburg Gotha was followed by the Windsors.

127 The capital of Tennessee is
☐ Knoxville
☐ Nashville
☐ Memphis.

128 Which of the following British authors does not belong to the so-called Angry Young Men of the 1950s?
☐ Kingsley Amis
☐ Ted Hughes
☐ Alan Sillitoe

129 'Albion' is
☐ an ancient name for Britain or England
☐ the name of a miraculous unicorn
☐ the name of one of the islands of the Outer Hebrides.

130 The Freedom Trail is in
☐ Lexington
☐ Boston
☐ Philadelphia.

Council House, Birmingham, UK.

The Royal Ascot is

131
☐ a fashionable British horse-racing event
☐ a popular boat race on the River Thames
☐ an annual meeting of the entire royal family.

Route 66 was the main road from

132
☐ Chicago to Los Angeles
☐ Detroit to San Francisco
☐ St Louis to Sacramento.

Newgate

133
☐ is the ancient town-gate of York.
☐ is the attractive new bridge in
    Newcastle-upon-Tyne.
☐ was a notorious prison in London.

The capital of Iowa is

134
☐ Cedar Rapids
☐ Davenport
☐ Des Moines.

Utopia (1516) was written by

135
☐ Sir Walter Raleigh
☐ Sir Francis Bacon
☐ Sir Thomas More.

136 Thomas Jefferson was the
☐ second
☐ third
☐ first
President of the United States.

137 In the British motion picture *Lawrence of Arabia* (1962), Thomas Edward Lawrence, an archaeological scholar and military strategist, supports
☐ the Arabs against the Turks
☐ the English against the Arabs
☐ the English against the Germans.

138 Which statement is not correct?
☐ The Pennsylvania Dutch lead a very strict and simple way of life.
☐ Their language is a form of German.
☐ They originally emigrated from different parts of the Netherlands.

139 'Adagio for Strings' (1938) is a famous short piece of music composed by
☐ Samuel Barber
☐ Charles Ives
☐ John Cage.

140 The Battle of the Boyne (1690) ended in
☐ a victory of English settlers over an Indian tribe in Massachusetts
☐ a victory of the British army over Indian rebels in Uttar Pradesh
☐ a victory in Ireland of King William III over the armies of the former King James II.

141 ☐ Wiltshire
☐ Derbyshire
☐ Warwickshire
does not belong to the Midlands.

142

Leaves of Grass (1855), a collection of poems that enlarged over the years, was written by
☐ Robert E. Lee
☐ Sidney Lanier
☐ Walt Whitman.

143

A condominium is
☐ a country belonging to the British Commonwealth.
☐ a special area in a zoo with different animals living together.
☐ a building containing apartments, each of which is owned by people living in it.

144

The Natural History Museum in London is near the
☐ Victoria & Albert Museum
☐ London Transport Museum
☐ Museum of Mankind.

145

The Ivy League is a group of
☐ the most highly respected universities in the north-eastern US
☐ the ten best US high schools
☐ the leading US baseball teams.

146

Barack Obama was Senator for
☐ Michigan
☐ Wisconsin
☐ Illinois.

147

The Spanish Armada, the greatest fleet of its time, was defeated by the English navy in
☐ 1577
☐ 1588
☐ 1599.

148

Cadbury World, an exhibition telling the story of chocolate, is situated in
☐ Stoke-on-Trent
☐ Manchester
☐ Birmingham.

149

The poem 'The Road Not Taken' was written by
- ☐ Robert Frost
- ☐ Carl Sandburg
- ☐ William Carlos Williams.

150

The main offices of the Boeing aircraft company are in
- ☐ Chicago
- ☐ Portland
- ☐ Seattle.

151

The All-England Championships are competitions in
- ☐ rugby
- ☐ cricket
- ☐ lawn tennis.

152

The film *Manhattan* (1978) was directed by
- ☐ Woody Allen
- ☐ Robert Benton
- ☐ John Cassavetes.

153

How many British kings called themselves George?
- ☐ eight
- ☐ six
- ☐ seven

154

The Dawes-Plan (1924) and the Young-Plan (1929)
- ☐ helped to unify secondary education in the USA.
- ☐ were initiated to stabilize the US dollar.
- ☐ were an arrangement for Germany's payment of reparations after World War I.

155

Motherwell is a town in
- ☐ Wales
- ☐ Scotland
- ☐ England.

Bagpipers in Inverness, Scotland.

Elizabeth Bennet is the central character in Jane Austen's novel

156
- [ ] *Sense and Sensibility* (1811)
- [ ] *Pride and Prejudice* (1813)
- [ ] *Persuasion* (1818).

The name of the largest city of New Mexico is spelled

157
- [ ] Albuquerque
- [ ] Albukerque
- [ ] Albuquerky.

Which statement is wrong?

158
- [ ] The Albert Memorial faces the Royal Albert Hall.
- [ ] The Churchill Memorial faces the Houses of Parliament.
- [ ] The Queen Victoria Memorial faces Buckingham Palace.

The first permanent community of English people in Virginia (1607) was

159
- [ ] Jamestown
- [ ] Yorktown
- [ ] Lancaster.

Southport is between

160
- [ ] Bolton and Blackburn
- [ ] Liverpool and Blackpool
- [ ] Sheffield and Huddersfield.

161
The play *Our Town* (1938) was written by
- ☐ Eugene O'Neill
- ☐ Thomas Wolfe
- ☐ Thornton Wilder.

162
CNN stands for
- ☐ Cable News Network
- ☐ Canadian News Network
- ☐ Campaign for Nature and Nurture.

163
Ely Cathedral is in
- ☐ Lincolnshire
- ☐ Leicestershire
- ☐ Cambridgeshire.

164
The imaginary person representing the US and its government is
- ☐ Uncle Tom
- ☐ Uncle Ben
- ☐ Uncle Sam.

165
Which of the following three was not a physicist?
- ☐ David Farragut
- ☐ Michael Faraday
- ☐ Daniel Gabriel Fahrenheit

166
The oldest underground railway in the USA is in
- ☐ New York
- ☐ Chicago
- ☐ Boston.

167
In London in the 1660s
- ☐ the Great Plague and the Great Fire happened at the same time.
- ☐ the Great Plague followed the Great Fire.
- ☐ the Great Plague preceded the Great Fire.

168
In which of these three US states is the capital identical with the largest city?
- ☐ Nebraska
- ☐ Michigan
- ☐ Rhode Island

169 Which statement about Geoffrey Chaucer's *Canterbury Tales* (1387ff.) is wrong?
☐ The storytellers are a cross-section of the English medieval society.
☐ The 23 stories are told in prose.
☐ The storytellers are pilgrims on their way from London to Canterbury.

170 The Big Easy is a popular name for the American city of
☐ New Orleans
☐ Jackson
☐ Mobile.

171 Poets' Corner in London is in
☐ St. Paul's Cathedral
☐ Westminster Abbey
☐ the British Library.

172 In the USA the Emmy Award is given
☐ for outstanding achievements in television
☐ to the best stage actors and actresses
☐ for the year's best pop songs.

173 The official abbreviation of London-City Airport is LCY. Which is it of Birmingham International Airport?
☐ BIA
☐ BHX
☐ BHM

174 The former capital of British India (1772 – 1912) was
☐ Delhi
☐ Bombay
☐ Calcutta.

175 Which states have a similar land area in square miles?
☐ Florida and Georgia
☐ New York State and New Mexico
☐ Oregon and Ohio

176 The first of Ian Fleming's 12 James Bond novels published in 1953 was
☐ *From Russia, with Love*
☐ *Dr No*
☐ *Casino Royale.*

177 Edward VII (King of Great Britain and Ireland from 1901 to 1910) was married to
☐ Queen Alexandra
☐ Queen Charlotte
☐ Queen Mary.

178 The movie *Gone with the Wind* was released in
☐ 1949
☐ 1945
☐ 1939.

179 Guy Fawkes (1570 – 1606) was
☐ a daring captain in Queen Elizabeth's navy
☐ one of the conspirators in the Gunpowder Plot
☐ a famous Tudor architect.

180 Miles Davis (1926 – 1991) was a famous American
☐ jazz singer
☐ pianist
☐ trumpeter.

181 Thomas Becket, at first friend and finally opponent of King Henry II, was murdered by four knights in 1170 in
☐ the Tower of London
☐ York Minster
☐ Canterbury Cathedral.

182 The capital of Colorado is
☐ Colorado Springs
☐ Pueblo
☐ Denver.

A San Francisco Cable Car.

Who wrote the series of 12 novels on the British naval officer Horatio Hornblower?

183
☐ Edward Morgan Forster
☐ William Edward Forster
☐ Cecil Scott Forester

The first consonant in 'Chicago' is pronounced in the same way as the first consonant in

184
☐ Chicano
☐ Chevrolet
☐ Chesterton.

Which of the following buildings was the tallest in the world in 1935?

185
☐ the Chrysler Building in NYC
☐ the Sears Tower in Chicago
☐ the Empire State Building in NYC

Which statement is wrong? - In the Australian flag

186
☐ there are six white stars
☐ one star is bigger than the others
☐ the Union Jack is in the top right corner.

Which of the three was a militant American Abolitionist, whose life and death (he was hanged in 1859) are commemorated in a famous song?

187
☐ James Brown
☐ Joseph Brown
☐ John Brown

188
The opponents in the Falklands War (1982) were
☐ Argentina and Chile
☐ England and Argentina
☐ England and Chile.

189
The biggest town in Suffolk is
☐ Harwich
☐ Colchester
☐ Ipswich.

190
The novel *Of Mice and Men* (1937) was written by
☐ Ernest Hemingway
☐ William Faulkner
☐ John Steinbeck.

191
Which of these large American airports has eight runways?
☐ O'Hare International Airport, Chicago
☐ Hartsfield-Jackson International Airport, Atlanta
☐ Los Angeles International Airport

192
Jack Charlton, an English football player, played for England and for
☐ West Ham United
☐ Leeds United
☐ Manchester United.

193
The main actor in the American movies *The Maltese Falcon* (1941), *The Big Sleep* (1946) and *African Queen* (1952) was
☐ Gary Cooper
☐ Humphrey Bogart
☐ Henry Fonda.

194
How long was Margaret Thatcher Prime Minister of the UK?
☐ eight years
☐ eleven years
☐ fourteen years

195

How many people were killed in the so-called Boston Massacre (March 5, 1770)?
- ☐ 500
- ☐ 5
- ☐ 50

196

The Brecon Beacons National Park is in the south of
- ☐ Scotland
- ☐ England
- ☐ Wales.

197

The religious novel *The Pilgrim's Progress* (1678 – 1684) was written by
- ☐ John Milton
- ☐ John Dryden
- ☐ John Bunyan.

198

Which spelling is correct?
- ☐ extasy
- ☐ ecstacy
- ☐ ecstasy

199

The Folger Shakespeare Library is in
- ☐ London
- ☐ Washington, D.C.
- ☐ New York.

200

The birthplace of President
- ☐ Lyndon B. Johnson
- ☐ John F. Kennedy
- ☐ James Earl Carter

is Brookline (near Boston).

201

What is the Eisteddfod?
- ☐ a Welsh competition for poets and musicians
- ☐ an annual meeting of Welsh bagpipe players
- ☐ a national holiday in Wales

202

The initials of the US organization in charge of
professional basketball are
☐ NBA
☐ NBC
☐ NBB.

203

Which family name does not appear twice in the
line of Presidents of the USA?
☐ Adams
☐ Truman
☐ Roosevelt

204

The ancient tribe of Caledonians lived in
☐ Wales
☐ Scotland
☐ Ireland.

205

Stratford-upon-Avon is in
☐ Staffordshire
☐ Avon
☐ Warwickshire.

206

Which of these novels begins with the words 'Call
me Ishmael.'?
☐ *The Scarlet Letter* (1850) by Nathaniel
  Hawthorne
☐ *Moby Dick* (1851) by Herman Melville
☐ *Walden* (1854) by Henry David Thoreau

207

The operetta *Candide* (1956) was composed by
☐ Aaron Copland
☐ Samuel Barber
☐ Leonard Bernstein.

208

Which of the following David-Lean-films is the
earliest one?
☐ *Dr Zhivago*
☐ *The Bridge on the River Kwai*
☐ *Lawrence of Arabia*

A rowing race on the River Cam in Cambridge, UK.

209

Which statement is wrong? The English Revolution of 1688 was called 'Glorious' because
- ☐ it was a crushing victory of William of Orange's army over that of James II
- ☐ it introduced constitutional monarchy
- ☐ the dethronement of King James II was bloodless.

210

Which statement is correct?
- ☐ The Hudson River flows through three US states.
- ☐ It touches the east side of Manhattan.
- ☐ It was named after an English navigator and explorer.

211

The musical *My Fair Lady* (1956) is based on Bernard Shaw's play
- ☐ *Major Barbara*
- ☐ *Candida*
- ☐ *Pygmalion*.

212

Which plural form is correct?
- ☐ sister-in-laws
- ☐ sisters-in-laws
- ☐ sisters-in-law

213

Trinity Church in Boston is near
- ☐ Beacon Street
- ☐ Commonwealth Avenue
- ☐ Boylston Street.

214

The FBI headquarters is in
☐ Washington, D.C.
☐ Baltimore
☐ New York City.

215

Which of the following has the third-longest reign in England (after Elizabeth II and Victoria)?
☐ Henry VIII
☐ Edward III
☐ George III

216

Who delivered the famous Gettysburg Address (November 19, 1863)?
☐ Robert E. Lee
☐ Abraham Lincoln
☐ Ulysses S. Grant

217

The Cayman Islands are in the
☐ Indian Ocean
☐ Pacific Ocean
☐ Caribbean Sea.

218

In Sir Arthur Conan Doyle's *A Study in Scarlet* (1887), Sherlock Holmes is introduced to Dr Watson who as an army surgeon served in
☐ Egypt
☐ Afghanistan
☐ Turkey.

219

When were the Rolling Stones formed as a pop group?
☐ 1966
☐ 1958
☐ 1962

220

The main role in *The French Connection* (1971) was played by
☐ Steve McQueen
☐ Gene Hackman
☐ Clint Eastwood.

221 What were Sir William Herschel (1738-1822, father) and Sir John Herschel (1792-1871, son) famous for?
- ☐ discoveries in astronomy
- ☐ experiments in chemistry
- ☐ explorations in geography

222 The London Underground station St. Paul's is served by
- ☐ the Circle Line
- ☐ the District Line
- ☐ the Central Line.

223 The United States of America entered the First World War in
- ☐ April 1917
- ☐ December 1916
- ☐ January 1918.

224 Marylebone Station in London is near
- ☐ Hyde Park
- ☐ Green Park
- ☐ Regent's Park.

225
- ☐ Charlotte
- ☐ Jane
- ☐ Emily

was not one of the Brontë sisters.

226 Which plural form is wrong?
- ☐ The Portugueses can easily adapt themselves abroad.
- ☐ In art I prefer still lifes.
- ☐ A lot of people lost their lives.

227 Columbia University in New York City is in
- ☐ the centre of Manhattan
- ☐ the north of Manhattan
- ☐ the south of Manhattan.

228
The ship in which Charles Darwin sailed to South America and the Galapagos Islands was
☐ HMS Beagle
☐ HMS Bounty
☐ HMS Endeavour.

229
The ferry between Liverpool and Dublin takes about
☐ eleven hours
☐ six hours
☐ nine hours.

230
Who was king of England when Joan of Arc (1412 – 1431) inspired the French against the English soldiers?
☐ Henry VI
☐ Richard II
☐ Henry IV

231
Which is the fourth largest city in the USA?
☐ Houston
☐ Philadelphia
☐ Phoenix

232
According to Agatha Christie, the master detective in many of her mystery tales, Hercule Poirot (occasionally misnamed 'Mr Porridge'), is
☐ Belgian
☐ French
☐ Luxemburg.

233
King James I of England (1603 – 1625) was also
☐ King James IV
☐ King James VI
☐ King James II
of Scotland.

234
A movie in Cinemascope is seen on a screen at the width-height-ratio of
☐ 3 : 1
☐ 2.55 : 1
☐ 3.25 : 1.5.

Skyscrapers in New York City.

235

'Al' in Al Capone (1899 – 1947), also called 'Scarface', is short for
☐ Alfred
☐ Alphonse
☐ Albert.

236

Who composed the suite *The Planets* (1920)?
☐ Ralph Vaughan Williams
☐ Frederick Delius
☐ Gustav Holst

237

The Hundred Years' War between England and France lasted
☐ more than 100 years
☐ less than 100 years
☐ exactly 100 years.

238

Which are called 'twin cities' in the USA?
☐ Birmingham and Montgomery
☐ St Paul and Minneapolis
☐ Austin and San Antonio

239

Who wrote the drama *The Spanish Tragedie* (1592)?
☐ John Marston
☐ Thomas Kyd
☐ Christopher Marlowe

240 Where do people speak Geordie, an accent very different from standard English?
- ☐ in the area around Glasgow
- ☐ in the area around Newcastle
- ☐ in the area around Blackpool

241 Which is not along 42nd Street/Manhattan?
- ☐ Times Square
- ☐ Grand Central Terminal
- ☐ Macy's

242 The CIA headquarters in Langley is in
- ☐ West Virginia
- ☐ Virginia
- ☐ North Carolina

243 Sir Edmund Hillary was born in
- ☐ Australia
- ☐ New Zealand
- ☐ England.

244 The Wars of the Roses (1455 – 1485) were
- ☐ a period of fighting between the House of Lancaster and the House of York
- ☐ hostilities between Gloucestershire and Buckinghamshire
- ☐ bloody conflicts between the sovereign and the House of Commons.

245 The largest county in England is
- ☐ Yorkshire
- ☐ Devon
- ☐ Lincolnshire.

246 Wystan Hugh Auden, Thomas Stearns Eliot and Henry James lived in England and the USA. Which of them was not born in America?
- ☐ James
- ☐ Auden
- ☐ Eliot

247 Edward Hopper (1882 – 1967) was a famous US
- ☐ photographer of industrial areas
- ☐ sculptor of the human body
- ☐ painter of realistic urban scenes.

248 Whose football ground is White Hart Lane in London?
- ☐ Queens Park Rangers
- ☐ Tottenham Hotspur
- ☐ FC Arsenal

249 Who was Rex Harrison's partner in the Broadway production of My Fair Lady, opened in 1956?
- ☐ Audrey Hepburn
- ☐ Julie Andrews
- ☐ Judy Garland

250 Which of the three was King Henry VIII's last wife?
- ☐ Catherine Parr
- ☐ Anne of Cleves
- ☐ Catherine Howard

251 What happened in the My Lai massacre of 1968?
- ☐ Over 300 civilians were killed by US soldiers.
- ☐ Over 300 American prisoners of war were killed by Viet Cong soldiers.
- ☐ Over 300 Viet Cong prisoners of war were killed by US soldiers.

252 Home Counties are
- ☐ all the counties in England
- ☐ the counties around London
- ☐ all the counties in Britain.

253 William Randolph Hearst (1863 – 1951) was an American
- ☐ newspaper publisher
- ☐ steel magnate
- ☐ bank manager.

254
Philately is the activity of collecting
☐ coins
☐ stamps
☐ medals.

255
Liberty Bell can be seen in
☐ Philadelphia
☐ Boston
☐ New York.

256
The US Medal of Honor is awarded to
☐ civilians who have done something special for
   the nation
☐ soldiers for special personal courage
☐ soldiers who are wounded in battle.

257
Who composed the ballet *Appalachian Spring* (1944)?
☐ Charles Ives
☐ George Gershwin
☐ Aaron Copland

258
Jesse Owens, Sir Roger Bannister and Bob Beamon were
☐ exceptionally successful athletes
☐ American athletes
☐ winners of Olympic gold medals.

259
The Danelaw was
☐ the hierarchy in the Danish invasion army
☐ the north-eastern part of England between the
   ninth and the eleventh centuries
☐ the set of laws and rules established in England
   by the Danish invaders.

260
In the English Channel the shortest distance between the English and the French coastlines is roughly
☐ 20 miles
☐ 15 miles
☐ 25 miles.

A typical village in the Cotswolds.

261 The novel *Finnegans Wake* (1939) was written by
☐ Virginia Woolf
☐ James Joyce
☐ David Herbert Lawrence.

262 Complete the following saying: 'Remember, remember the
☐ last
☐ first
☐ fifth
of November.'

263 In the US TV series *Kojak*, Lieutenant Kojak's Christian name is
☐ Lew
☐ Theo
☐ Ed.

264 Speeches and debates in the British parliament are published daily in
☐ Parliament Today
☐ Hansard
☐ Parliament Proceedings.

265 Chief Joseph (1840 – 1904) was chief of the
☐ Cherokee
☐ Seminole
☐ Nez Percé.

266 Which statement is wrong? King Richard I (the
Lionheart, 1157 – 1199)
☐ took part in the First Crusade.
☐ was captured and held prisoner in Austria.
☐ was succeeded by his brother John.

267 The Grampian Mountains are in
☐ north-west Wales
☐ central Scotland
☐ the Lake District.

268 The novel *The Vicar of Wakefield* (1766) was
written by
☐ Laurence Sterne
☐ Oliver Goldsmith
☐ Henry Fielding.

269 The pianist Glenn Gould (1932 – 1982) was
☐ British
☐ American
☐ Canadian.

270 Boris Karloff (1887 – 1969) played the main role in
the horror movie
☐ *Dracula* (1931)
☐ *Dr. Jekyll and Mr. Hyde* (1932)
☐ *Frankenstein* (1931).

271 Alfred Charles Kinsey (1894 – 1956) investigated
☐ the habitats of chimpanzees
☐ human sexual behaviour
☐ the long-term effects of thermonuclear
explosions.

272 The Forth Road Bridge was built
☐ at almost the same time as the Forth Railroad
Bridge
☐ way after the Forth Railroad Bridge
☐ way before the Forth Railroad Bridge.

273

The Boston Tea Party occurred in
☐ 1775
☐ 1771
☐ 1773.

274

The total area of the United Kingdom is
☐ two and a half
☐ three and a half
☐ four and a half
times as large as the total area of the Republic of
Ireland.

275

Thomas Bowdler's *Family Shakespeare* (1818) is
a/an
☐ simplified
☐ expurgated
☐ shortened
version of Shakespeare's plays.

276

'Laparoscopy' is
☐ the scientific analysis of minerals
☐ the visual examination of the abdominal cavity
by means of an endoscope
☐ an analysis by extreme magnification.

277

Lambeth Palace in London is
☐ the London house of the archbishop of
Canterbury
☐ Prince Edward's residence
☐ one of the numerous museums.

278

Labor Day (a national holiday) in the USA is on
☐ the first Monday in September
☐ the first of May
☐ the first Thursday in October.

279

The time of action in Aldous Huxley's novel *Brave
New World* (1932) is the year
☐ 2600 A.D.
☐ A.F. 632
☐ 2350.

280
La Guardia Airport in New York City was named
after Fiorello Henry La Guardia (1882 – 1947), who
☐ was an influential American architect.
☐ was US Minister of Transport.
☐ served as Mayor of New York City three times.

281
Stornoway is a town on one of the islands of the
☐ Orkney Islands
☐ Inner Hebrides
☐ Outer Hebrides.

282
Which is correct? In the chronology of Shakespeare's
plays
☐ *Othello* is before *The Tempest*
☐ *Richard III* is after *Julius Caesar*
☐ *Hamlet* is after *Macbeth.*

283
Which of the Kennedy brothers was assassinated in
1968?
☐ John F.
☐ Robert F.
☐ Edward

284
Which is correct? The role of Agent 007 – James
Bond – was played by
☐ Pierce Brosnan (three times)
☐ Sir Roger Moore (seven times)
☐ Sir Sean Connery (five times).

285
Edith Head (1898 – 1981) was
☐ a script writer for the MGM film studios
☐ an editor for Columbia Pictures
☐ America's most successful motion picture
   costume designer.

286
The US pop singer and actress Madonna was born in
☐ 1964
☐ 1952
☐ 1958.

The Chicago Theater on North State Street, Chicago.

287

In the Vietnam War US forces sprayed Agent Orange
☐ to burn down fortified Viet Cong positions.
☐ to defoliate forest areas and to destroy crops.
☐ to paralyse enemy troops.

288

Of the five Great Lakes
☐ Lake Michigan
☐ Lake Superior
☐ Lake Ontario
is the most northern one.

289

The play *The Glass Menagerie* (1945) was written by
☐ Tennessee Williams
☐ Thornton Wilder
☐ Arthur Miller.

290

In the Battle at the Alamo (1836) 187 Texans were
killed by
☐ a superior force of Native Americans
☐ British troops
☐ 4000 Mexican soldiers.

291

The replica of the Globe Theatre in London is
- ☐ on the north bank of the Thames
- ☐ near Tate Modern
- ☐ south of the National Theatre.

292

Which statement on long measures is wrong?
- ☐ A fathom is six feet long.
- ☐ A furlong is one eighth of a mile long.
- ☐ A league is four miles long.

293

Inigo Jones, Sir Christopher Wren and Frank Lloyd Wright were
- ☐ British
- ☐ architects
- ☐ poets.

294

Together with the Prussian army
- ☐ the Duke of Marlborough
- ☐ the Duke of Wellington
- ☐ Lord Nelson

defeated Napoleon's army in the Battle of Waterloo (1815).

295

The capital of Illinois is
- ☐ Springfield
- ☐ Chicago
- ☐ Peoria.

296

James Jones' novel *From Here to Eternity* (1951) is about
- ☐ the landing of the Allies in Normandy (6 June 1944)
- ☐ US army life in Pearl Harbor before the Japanese attack (7 December 1941)
- ☐ the Battle of Midway (June 1942).

297

Dr Martin Luther King (1929 – 1968), the most outstanding leader of the US Civil Rights Movement in the 1950s and 1960s, was by profession a
- ☐ physician
- ☐ Baptist minister
- ☐ lawyer.

298 Sir Matthew (Matt) Busby (1909 – 1994) was
☐ the manager of Manchester United
☐ the director of the British Museum
☐ a minister in Margaret Thatcher's cabinet.

299 Whose original name was Archibald Alexander Leach (1904 – 1986)?
☐ David Niven
☐ Cary Grant
☐ Stewart Granger

300 Which statement is wrong?
☐ Elizabeth I gave the order to have Lady Jane Grey beheaded.
☐ Lady Jane Grey was executed at the age of 16.
☐ Lady Jane Grey was Queen of England for nine days.

301 Chequers, a large house in Buckinghamshire, is the official country home of
☐ the British Prime Minister
☐ the Archbishop of Canterbury
☐ the Secretary of State for Defence.

302 Which of the following was a contemporary of Shakespeare's?
☐ Gerald Ford
☐ John Ford
☐ Ford Madox Ford

303 The Royal Armouries, a museum displaying weapons of all sorts and ages, is in
☐ Liverpool
☐ London
☐ Leeds.

304 Emmeline Pankhurst (1858 - 1928) was
☐ the first Englishwoman to run a large company
☐ an English suffragette leader
☐ a famous opera soprano.

305

The film version of the musical *The Sound of Music* (1965) stars
☐ Julie Andrews and Christopher Plummer
☐ Audrey Hepburn and Sir Rex Harrison
☐ Liza Minnelli and Danny Kaye.

306

In the House of Lords the Lord Chancellor resides over debates on
☐ a gilded armchair
☐ an elevated seat
☐ a woolsack.

307

In the film *The Odd Couple* (1967) Jack Lemmon appeared with
☐ Tony Curtis
☐ Dean Martin
☐ Walter Matthau.

308

Sorority is
☐ a club for male students at some US colleges and universities
☐ a club for female students at some US colleges and universities
☐ an organization supporting women's emancipation in the USA.

309

The Admiralty Arch in London is near
☐ Trafalgar Square
☐ the Imperial War Museum
☐ the Temple.

310

The US government organization that gathers information and does research on foreign governments and operations is the
☐ FBI
☐ CIA
☐ CID.

Tower Bridge across the Thames, a landmark of London.

311 Geoffrey Chaucer, whose best-known work is *The Canterbury Tales*, lived in
☐ the 16th century
☐ the 14th century
☐ the 15th century.

312 US actor Henry Fonda (1905 – 1982) is the father of
☐ Peter and Jane Fonda
☐ Peter and Janet Fonda
☐ Patrick and Jane Fonda.

313 *Tinker, Sailor, Soldier, Spy* (1974) was written by
☐ Ian Fleming
☐ Len Deighton
☐ John le Carré.

314 Pancake Day in Britain is on
☐ Wednesday
☐ Monday
☐ Tuesday.

315 The Solomon Islands, a British protectorate from the 1890s to 1978, are in
☐ the Atlantic Ocean
☐ the Pacific Ocean
☐ the Indian Ocean.

316

In the second Act of Union (1800)
☐ Great Britain and Ireland
☐ England and Scotland
☐ England and Wales
were joined.

317

The Hitchhiker's Guide to the Galaxy (1979) was
written by
☐ Douglas
☐ Gerry
☐ John
Adams.

318

The range of hills between London and Oxford are
called
☐ the Cotswolds
☐ the Cheviots
☐ the Chilterns.

319

In Texas,
☐ Dallas and Wichita Falls
☐ Fort Worth and Dallas
☐ Houston and Austin
are neighbouring cities.

320

John Lennon, English singer and guitar player with
the Beatles, was murdered
☐ in Los Angeles in 1985
☐ in London in 1975
☐ in New York City in 1980.

321

The Dorchester, an expensive hotel in London, is in
☐ Park Way
☐ Park Avenue
☐ Park Lane.

322

A 'penny-farthing' was
☐ a type of bicycle in the late 19th century
☐ one twelfth of a florin
☐ a British coin in the late 18th century.

323
Captain Robert F. Scott (1868 – 1912) died on an expedition
☐ trying to find the Northwest Passage
☐ to the North Pole
☐ to the Antarctic.

324
'Scouse' is the way of speaking that is typical of people from
☐ Sheffield
☐ Liverpool
☐ Southampton.

325
In Hemingway's novel *For Whom the Bell Tolls* (1940) the action is set in
☐ Spain
☐ Portugal
☐ Italy.

326
In the 1980s Olympics, Carl Lewis won gold medals
☐ in the 100-metre and the long jump
☐ in the 100-metre and the high jump
☐ in the decathlon.

327
The British Prime Minister
☐ Stanley Baldwin
☐ Neville Chamberlain
☐ Clement Attlee
signed the Munich Agreement/Pact in September 1938.

328
The initials in the name of the English novelist D.H. Lawrence (1885 – 1930) stand for
☐ Daniel Herbert
☐ David Henry
☐ David Herbert.

329
Liberace (1919 – 1987) was a US
☐ Mafia boss
☐ fashion designer
☐ piano player and singer.

330

In the very popular US comic strip *Peanuts* Charly Brown's dog is called
☐ Snoopy
☐ Lucy
☐ Linus.

331

The capital of Sri Lanka, once a colony in the British Empire, is
☐ Ceylon
☐ Antananarivo
☐ Colombo.

332

The Aldeburgh Festival was created by
☐ Michael Tippett
☐ Benjamin Britten
☐ Malcolm Arnold.

333

Which of the three US films was the most expensive one?
☐ *The Ten Commandments* (1956)
☐ *Gone With the Wind* (1939)
☐ *Cleopatra* (1963)

334

The poets
☐ S.T. Coleridge and W. Wordsworth
☐ T.S. Eliot and J. Masefield
☐ A. Tennyson and R. Browning
were R. Southey's contemporaries.

335

The Adirondack Mountains are in the US state of
☐ Nebraska
☐ New York
☐ Utah.

336

Who is commemorated in a statue in front of Elland Road Football Stadium in Leeds?
☐ Don Revie
☐ Billy Bremner
☐ Jack Charlton

St Pancras International Station, London, UK.

337

The detective novel *The Mysterious Affair at Styles* (1920) was written by
☐ Margery Allingham
☐ Gilbert Keith Chesterton
☐ Agatha Christie.

338

At Fort Sumter
☐ the American Civil War (1861 – 1865) began.
☐ the California Gold Rush (1848/9) began.
☐ the Mexican War (1846 – 1848) between the US and Mexico began.

339

Which were not a pair of comic actors?
☐ Nicola Sacco, Bartolomeo Vanzetti
☐ Bud Abbot, Lou Costello
☐ Stan Laurel, Oliver Hardy

340

In 1966, a large pile of coal waste fell onto a school, killing 116 children and 28 adults in the Welsh town of
☐ Abergavenny
☐ Aberfan
☐ Aberystwyth.

341

☐ George Cukor
☐ John Ford
☐ Fred Zinnemann
directed the US western *High Noon* (1952).

342 Abbotsford, a large house near the River Tweed in
Scotland, was built for
☐ Sir Walter Scott
☐ Robert Burns
☐ Robert Louis Stevenson.

343 South Glamorgan is a county in
☐ Scotland
☐ Ireland
☐ Wales.

344 The Grand National, a famous British horse race, is
held at Aintree near
☐ Liverpool
☐ Nottingham
☐ Oxford.

345 The US film *Citizen Kane* (1941) is based on the
life of
☐ Lionel Nathan Rothschild
☐ William Randolph Hearst
☐ John Davison Rockefeller.

346 Mahatma
☐ Ghandi
☐ Gandhi
☐ Gandi
helped India become independent in 1947.

347 Which of the three is the largest natural lake?
☐ Lake Superior
☐ Lake Victoria
☐ Lake Huron

348 ☐ The Founding Fathers
☐ The Pioneer Fathers
☐ The Pilgrim Fathers
created and signed the American Constitution in
Philadelphia in 1787.

349 The song 'Alexander's Ragtime Band' was composed by
- ☐ Irving Berlin
- ☐ Frederick Loewe
- ☐ George Gershwin.

350 The old-fashioned term 'bobby' (= policeman) goes back to Prime Minister
- ☐ Sir Robert Walpole
- ☐ William Pitt
- ☐ Sir Robert Peel.

351 Stamford Bridge is not
- ☐ a village in north-east England
- ☐ a football stadium in London
- ☐ a bridge across the Thames in London.

352 Who is not a US actress?
- ☐ Glenn Close
- ☐ Meryl Streep
- ☐ Nicole Kidman

353 Which statement about the Golden Gate Bridge is wrong?
- ☐ It takes four years to paint.
- ☐ It connects San Francisco with Santa Cruz.
- ☐ It was completed in 1937.

354 Roy Lichtenstein (1923 – 1997) was
- ☐ a British
- ☐ an American
- ☐ a Canadian

painter and representative of pop art.

355 The Pentagon is in
- ☐ Arlington, Virginia
- ☐ Washington D.C.
- ☐ Raleigh, North Carolina.

356

The oldest university in Scotland is in
☐ St Andrews
☐ Glasgow
☐ Edinburgh.

357

Which statement about King Alfred the Great is
wrong?
☐ He fought against the Normans.
☐ He belonged to the House of Wessex.
☐ He fought against the Danes.

358

The popular US novel *Gone With the Wind* (1936)
was written by
☐ Margaret Mitchell
☐ Harriet Beecher Stowe
☐ Catherine Cookson.

359

Perpendicular, a style of architecture, was used in
England in the
☐ late Renaissance
☐ 14th and 15th centuries
☐ early 19th century.

360

In Jonathan Swift's *Gulliver's Travels* (1726), the
hero, Lemuel Gulliver, visits the giants of Brobding-
nag on his
☐ first
☐ third
☐ second
travel.

361

The postal abbreviation of Mississippi is
☐ MP
☐ MS
☐ MI.

362

The America's Cup is an international contest in
☐ sailing
☐ golf
☐ hockey.

A view of London and the River Thames.

363 Sir Arthur Conan Doyle was a
☐ historian
☐ lawyer
☐ doctor
before he began writing his Holmes stories.

364 ☐ Spike Milligan
☐ Peter Sellers
☐ Michael Palin
was not a member of the Goon Show broadcast by
the BBC in the 1950s.

365 In Charles Dickens's *Little Dorrit* William Dorrit is
in
☐ Pentonville prison
☐ Marshalsea prison
☐ Newgate prison.

366 Allan Pinkerton (1819 – 1884) established
☐ the first US company of private detectives
☐ a large company producing glass products
☐ an influential news agency.

367 The capital of Michigan is
☐ Grand Rapids
☐ Lansing
☐ Detroit.

368 The airport near Liverpool is called
☐ Mersey International Airport
☐ Liverpool John Lennon Airport
☐ Speke Airport.

369

Which statement is wrong?
- ☐ Sutton Hoo is a historic village in Lincoln.
- ☐ In Sutton Hoo an Anglo-Saxon ship was found in 1939.
- ☐ The treasure of Sutton Hoo is now in the British Museum.

370

'The Rime of the Ancient Mariner' (1798) is a long poem by
- ☐ Robert Southey
- ☐ William Wordsworth
- ☐ Samuel Taylor Coleridge.

371

Queen Elizabeth II keeps
- ☐ beagles
- ☐ spaniels
- ☐ corgis

as pets.

372

Which of the following Scottish lakes is the most northern one?
- ☐ Loch Katrine
- ☐ Loch Tay
- ☐ Loch Lomond

373

Which of the three singers was not born in 1958?
- ☐ Janet Jackson
- ☐ Prince
- ☐ Michael Jackson

374

The best-known railway station in the USA is not called
- ☐ New York Central Station
- ☐ Grand Central Station
- ☐ Grand Central Terminal.

375

Which statement is wrong? David Livingstone (1813 – 1873)
- ☐ was found by Henry Morton Stanley in Africa.
- ☐ was the first European to see the Victoria Falls in 1855.
- ☐ tried to find Henry Morton Stanley in Africa.

376
The British group
☐ The Rolling Stones
☐ Pink Floyd
☐ Queen
published the album 'The Wall' in 1979.

377
The 'Swan of Avon' was a nickname for
☐ Christopher Marlowe
☐ Ben Jonson
☐ William Shakespeare.

378
Goodison Park is a football ground in
☐ Manchester
☐ London
☐ Liverpool.

379
The three Anglo-Dutch Wars were fought in the
☐ 17th century
☐ 18th century
☐ 16th century.

380
The British TV soap opera *Coronation Street*
(started in 1960) is set in
☐ Coventry
☐ Newcastle
☐ Manchester.

381
The Grand Union Canal, the longest canal in
Britain, is between
☐ Bristol and Southampton
☐ London and Birmingham
☐ York and Nottingham.

382
The philosophical work *An Essay Concerning
Human Understanding* (1690) was written by
☐ John Locke
☐ Thomas Hobbes
☐ Adam Smith.

383
The sailors who took part in the mutiny on the
Bounty (1789) occupied one of the
☐ Pitcairn Islands
☐ Society Islands
☐ Marquesas Islands.

384
Thomas Tallis (1505 – 1585) was
☐ a member of the Gunpowder Plot
☐ a composer of mainly religious music
☐ the Archbishop of Canterbury.

385
Which statement is wrong? Princess Anne
☐ was born in 1950.
☐ was given the title of Princess Royal in 1987.
☐ was divorced from her first husband, Timothy
Laurence, in 1992.

386
Which of these states does not belong to the
so-called Cotton Belt in the USA?
☐ Oklahoma
☐ Georgia
☐ Indiana

387
The Grapes of Wrath (1939) was written by
☐ John Steinbeck
☐ Sinclair Lewis
☐ Thornton Wilder.

388
In 1988 a bomb explosion killed 270 people above
and on the ground of
☐ Dumfries
☐ Lockerbie
☐ Longtown.

389
The youngest man ever to become Prime Minister
of Britain (at 24) was
☐ Stanley Baldwin
☐ William Pitt
☐ Benjamin Disraeli.

A canal in Birmingham, UK.

390 The Tardis is
☐ a mountain in Northern Scotland
☐ a medieval musical instrument
☐ the vehicle in which Dr Who travels through space and time in a British TV series.

391 Who sings the song 'I'm an ordinary man' in the musical *My Fair Lady* (1956)?
☐ Professor Henry Higgins
☐ Alfred P. Doolittle
☐ Colonel Pickering

392 Who followed Queen Anne (1665 – 1714) on the English throne?
☐ Queen Mary II
☐ King George I
☐ King William III

393 The Courtauld Institute is
☐ a physics department at Cambridge University
☐ an art gallery in London
☐ a government institute to explore poverty in the UK.

394 The poem 'Elegy Written in a Country Churchyard' (1751) was written by
☐ Alexander Pope
☐ Horace Walpole
☐ Thomas Gray.

395

The only bridge crossing the Thames in London until 1750 was
☐ London Bridge
☐ Southwark Bridge
☐ Blackfriars Bridge.

396

Plaid Cymru is
☐ the Welsh nationalist political party
☐ an old theatre in Edinburgh
☐ a medium-sized town in the Republic of Ireland.

397

Edward Teller (1908 – 2003)
☐ was Governor of Virginia.
☐ co-created the first hydrogen bomb.
☐ designed futuristic furniture.

398

'The Gunners' is the nickname of the London football club
☐ Tottenham Hotspur
☐ Queens Park Rangers
☐ Arsenal.

399

Which statement about Covent Garden is wrong?
☐ It is a popular park in London.
☐ It is another name for the Royal Opera House.
☐ It is a market square filled with small shops and restaurants.

400

The world's first international trade fair, the Great Exhibition, took place in the Crystal Palace in
☐ Manchester
☐ London
☐ Birmingham.

401

Which of the following initials is not mainly connected with classical music in London?
☐ LSO
☐ LSE
☐ LPO

402 Which statement about Pocahontas is wrong?
- ☐ She later called herself Rebecca.
- ☐ She married Captain John Smith.
- ☐ She went to England in 1616.

403 The Temple in London is
- ☐ a Catholic church in the City
- ☐ an 18th century art gallery
- ☐ a group of buildings where lawyers work or are trained.

404 The Artful Dodger is a thief in a novel by
- ☐ Charles Dickens
- ☐ William Makepeace Thackeray
- ☐ Thomas Hardy.

405 The traditional British 'cream tea' consists of tea, clotted cream, jam and
- ☐ rolls
- ☐ scones
- ☐ longish cakes.

406 Kate Greenaway (1846 – 1901)
- ☐ wrote children's books.
- ☐ illustrated children's books.
- ☐ collected and published nursery rhymes.

407 When Oliver Cromwell (1599 – 1658) ruled England, Scotland and Ireland in the 1650s, he had the title
- ☐ Lord Protector
- ☐ Lord Chancellor
- ☐ Lord Chamberlain.

408 Sidney Poitier (b. 1927) won an Oscar for his part in
- ☐ *Lilies of the Field* (1963)
- ☐ *Porgy and Bess* (1959)
- ☐ *In the Heat of the Night* (1967).

409

The first line of the traditional song 'Ten Green Bottles' says 'Ten green bottles
- ☐ hanging
- ☐ swinging
- ☐ dangling

on the wall ... '.

410

The legendary King Arthur is said to have fought against the
- ☐ Danes
- ☐ Normans
- ☐ Saxons.

411

Francis Crick (1916 – 2004) and James Watson (b. 1928)
- ☐ cooperated on the Manhattan Project.
- ☐ were astronomers at the Jodrell Bank laboratories.
- ☐ worked on the discovery of DNA structure.

412

The famous English song 'Greensleeves' is about
- ☐ Robin Hood's Lincoln green (= garment)
- ☐ unrequited love
- ☐ the natural wonder of green landscapes.

413

Which of the statements about J.R.R. Tolkien's *The Lord of the Rings* (1954f.) is wrong?
- ☐ Each of the three parts consists of three books.
- ☐ The second part is entitled *The Two Towers*.
- ☐ *The Hobbit* was written before *The Lord of the Rings*.

414

The Pony Express was
- ☐ the US mail service from 1860 to 1861, using riders and horses
- ☐ the first passenger train in the USA
- ☐ the first tourist train in Disneyland (Anaheim, California).

The Forth Bridge across the Firth of Forth, a UNESCO World Heritage Site in Scotland.

415
- ☐ *1066 And All That*
- ☐ *1066 And After*
- ☐ *1066 And The Battle Of Britain*

is a humorous book about the history of Britain.

416
The Maori in New Zealand originally came from
- ☐ Tasmania
- ☐ Western Australia
- ☐ Polynesia.

417
Arthur Ashe (1943 – 1993) was an American
- ☐ track and field athlete
- ☐ ballet dancer
- ☐ tennis player.

418
The Cuban missile crisis between the USA and the USSR was in
- ☐ 1960
- ☐ 1962
- ☐ 1964.

419
The National Maritime Museum is in
- ☐ Southend-on-Sea
- ☐ Greenwich, London
- ☐ Plymouth.

420

Lord's is
- ☐ a cricket ground in London
- ☐ a London firm of auctioneers
- ☐ a short form of the House of Lords.

421

In Britain, the day on which people commemorate the dead of the two world wars is not called
- ☐ Remembrance Sunday
- ☐ Veterans' Day
- ☐ Poppy Day.

422

Which of the following states does not border Texas?
- ☐ Missouri
- ☐ New Mexico
- ☐ Louisiana

423

The Ashmolean Museum (opened in 1683), the oldest public museum in Britain, is in
- ☐ Bath
- ☐ Oxford
- ☐ Bristol.

424

Which statement about the Battle of Culloden (1746) is wrong?
- ☐ The battlefield was near Fort William.
- ☐ It was fought between mainly English soldiers and the Scottish army.
- ☐ It was the last battle to be fought in Britain.

425

In 1821 the national newspaper The Guardian was started in
- ☐ Manchester
- ☐ London
- ☐ Liverpool.

426

Los Alamos, where the first atomic and hydrogen bombs were developed, is a small town in
- ☐ New Mexico
- ☐ Texas
- ☐ Arizona.

427 Portland cement was invented in the early 19th century
☐ in Portland, Oregon
☐ on the Isle of Portland, Dorset
☐ in Portland, Maine.

428 Margaret Thatcher (1925 – 2013) was a
☐ physicist
☐ chemist and barrister
☐ journalist
before she went into politics.

429 Which is not a news agency?
☐ RMT
☐ AP
☐ Reuters

430 General George Custer was killed in
☐ the Battle at the Alamo (1836)
☐ the Battle of Little Bighorn (1876)
☐ the Mexican War (1846).

431 The furthest north of the Channel Islands is
☐ Alderney
☐ Jersey
☐ Guernsey.

432 The Guilford Four, The Birmingham Six and The Maguire Seven were
☐ Irishmen wrongly accused and imprisoned
☐ notorious drug gangs
☐ very successful entrepreneurs.

433 The largest lake in the British Isles is
☐ Lough Ree
☐ Loch Ness
☐ Lough Neagh.

434 Portobello Road in London is in
☐ Bayswater
☐ Kensington
☐ Notting Hill.

435 Finish the first line of a well-known nursery rhyme:
'There was an old woman who lived in a ...'
- [ ] shop
- [ ] shed
- [ ] shoe.'

436 Aston University is in
- [ ] Leicester
- [ ] Birmingham
- [ ] Coventry.

437 The Cutty Sark, a famous British sailing ship, is open to visitors in
- [ ] London
- [ ] Plymouth
- [ ] Portsmouth.

438 The Massachusetts Institute of Technology (MIT) is in
- [ ] Brookline
- [ ] Boston
- [ ] Cambridge.

439 The first British football player to be knighted (1965) was
- [ ] Stanley Matthews
- [ ] Danny Blanchflower
- [ ] Bobby Charlton.

440 The Mauna Kea Observatory is on
- [ ] Oahu
- [ ] Maui
- [ ] Hawaii.

441 The 1996 Olympic Games were held in
- [ ] Atlanta
- [ ] Los Angeles
- [ ] Chicago.

The United States Capitol in Washington, D.C.

The US organization supporting the use of guns for
hunting, sport and self-defence is called

442
- ☐ NRLB
- ☐ NLRB
- ☐ NRA.

The Luddites were opposed to

443
- ☐ English intervention in Ireland
- ☐ the reign of Queen Elizabeth I
- ☐ the introduction of new machines or technology.

The disastrous potato famine in Ireland happened
between

444
- ☐ 1845 and 1847
- ☐ 1832 and 1835
- ☐ 1856 and 1859.

445
- ☐ Joseph Mallord William Turner
- ☐ Thomas Gainsborough
- ☐ Sir Joshua Reynolds

is famous for his seascape paintings with his original
treatment of light and weather conditions.

446
- ☐ Pennsylvania
- ☐ Rhode Island
- ☐ Kentucky

was not one of the first 13 US states in 1776.

John James Audubon (1785 – 1851)
☐ was a minister in President Zachary Taylor's
   cabinet.

447

☐ painted every bird then known in North
   America for his book Birds of America.
☐ was a leading representative of the Mormons.

The poem 'Daffodils' was written by
☐ John Keats

448

☐ Samuel Taylor Coleridge
☐ William Wordsworth.

Haggis is a famous
☐ Scottish

449

☐ Welsh
☐ Irish
dish.

Which statement is wrong? In Shakespeare's *Macbeth* (1606), the hero is instigated to kill the king by
☐ Banquo, one of his comrades in arms

450

☐ Lady Macbeth
☐ his own ambition.

☐ The Susquehanna River
☐ The Shenandoah River

451

☐ The Potomac River
flows through Washington, D.C.

In the 1980 and 1984 Olympic Games, Daley Thompson (GB; b. 1958) won gold medals in
☐ the decathlon

452

☐ the 400 metres hurdles
☐ the long jump.

The novel *Emma* (1816) was written by
☐ Charlotte Brontë

453

☐ Jane Austen
☐ Mary Wollstonecraft Shelley.

454

Between 1013 and 1042 England was ruled by the
- ☐ Angles and Saxons
- ☐ Normans
- ☐ Danes.

455

Although married to Sir William, Lady Emma Hamilton fell in love with
- ☐ the Duke of Marlborough
- ☐ Lord Nelson
- ☐ the Duke of Wellington.

456

The most northern of the New England States is
- ☐ Vermont
- ☐ Maine
- ☐ New Hampshire.

457

The US pop singer and guitar player Elvis Presley died at the age of
- ☐ 42
- ☐ 47
- ☐ 38.

458

Tin Lizzie was
- ☐ a pilot's pet name for a World War I fighter aircraft
- ☐ a popular name for the Model T car
- ☐ a nickname for the actress Elizabeth Taylor.

459

The Authorized Version, an English translation of the Bible, was ordered by King
- ☐ James I
- ☐ Charles II
- ☐ Henry VIII.

460

Which of these English cities on the coast is the most southern one?
- ☐ Southampton
- ☐ Plymouth
- ☐ Portsmouth

461
Which statement about Charles Darwin (1809 – 1882) is wrong?
- ☐ He studied animals and plants on the Galapagos Islands.
- ☐ During this expedition he travelled on board the Beagle.
- ☐ In 1859 he published *On the Origin of Species by Means of Evolution*.

462
A leader of the American Revolution of 1776 was
- ☐ John Hancock
- ☐ Tony Hancock
- ☐ Herbie Hancock.

463
In Richard Brinsley Sheridan's play *The Rivals* (1775) Mrs Malaprop
- ☐ tries to hatch an intrigue.
- ☐ tries to make a gentleman fall in love with her.
- ☐ has the tendency to confuse words that sound similar.

464
Sir Michael Tippett (1905 – 1998) was
- ☐ a Conservative MP
- ☐ the vice-chancellor of Oxford University
- ☐ a composer of classical music.

465
John Boynton Priestley (1894 – 1984) wrote his play *An Inspector Calls* (1946) within a
- ☐ week
- ☐ year
- ☐ month.

466
The patron saint of Wales is
- ☐ St Andrew
- ☐ St Patrick
- ☐ St David.

467
In the legend of King Arthur dead heroes are taken to
- ☐ Camelot
- ☐ Tintagel
- ☐ Avalon.

The Golden Gate Bridge, carrying U.S. Route 101 across the San Francisco Bay.

468 Harlem, a district of north Manhattan in New York City, was originally a
☐ German
☐ Belgian
☐ Dutch
village.

469 The two official languages on Malta are
☐ Maltese and Italian
☐ English and Maltese
☐ English and Italian.

470 There have been Prime Ministers of Great Britain since the
☐ 1720s
☐ 1830s
☐ 1770s.

471 Whose original name was Norma Jean Baker?
☐ Judy Garland
☐ Marilyn Monroe
☐ Bette Davis

472

'The Backs'
- [ ] is the area between the River Cam and some colleges of Cambridge University
- [ ] is the large park behind Buckingham Palace
- [ ] is a district in Boston (Mass.).

473

Henry Moore (1898 – 1986) is famous for his
- [ ] paintings
- [ ] sculptures
- [ ] architecture.

474

The capital of Ohio is
- [ ] Cleveland
- [ ] Toledo
- [ ] Columbus.

475

Which two football clubs are not in the same city?
- [ ] Queen's Park Rangers and Aston Villa
- [ ] FC Liverpool and FC Everton
- [ ] Tottenham Hotspur and West Ham United

476

Harley Street in central London is famous for its
- [ ] exclusive shops
- [ ] luxurious hotels
- [ ] clinics and medical practices.

477

If you happen to meet Queen Elizabeth II, you address her with
- [ ] Your Majesty
- [ ] Your Excellency
- [ ] Your Highness.

478

The Manhattan Project was the idea
- [ ] to link art and science.
- [ ] to erect skyscrapers in New York City.
- [ ] to develop the atom bomb.

479

Who won an Oscar for the music of the film *Purple Rain* (1984)?
- [ ] Freddie Mercury
- [ ] Prince
- [ ] Michael Jackson

William Shakespeare's *Titus Andronicus* (1591) is
set in ancient

480
☐ Carthage
☐ Athens
☐ Rome.

The most populous of all Indian groups in the
United States are the

481
☐ Apache
☐ Cheyenne
☐ Navajo.

Which of the following was a painter?

482
☐ Francis Bacon (1561 – 1626)
☐ Roger Bacon (1214 – 1292)
☐ Francis Bacon (1909 – 1992)

The last Anglo-Saxon king of England was

483
☐ Edward (the Confessor)
☐ Canute
☐ Harold II.

Mardi Gras is a popular US carnival during the
week before

484
☐ Easter
☐ Ash Wednesday
☐ Thanksgiving Day.

Prospero is the leading character in Shakespeare's
play

485
☐ *Love's Labour's Lost*
☐ *Much Ado About Nothing*
☐ *The Tempest.*

How many colonies declared themselves independent
of Britain in 1776?

486
☐ 10
☐ 16
☐ 13

487 J.R.R. Tolkien (1882 – 1973) wrote *The Hobbit* and *The Lord of the Rings.* His initials stand for
☐ Joseph Ronald Rufus
☐ John Randall Royce
☐ John Ronald Reuel.

488 Harvard, the oldest US university, was established in
☐ 1718
☐ 1636
☐ 1572.

489 Sherlock Holmes, the private detective in Sir Arthur Conan Doyle's stories, lives in London in Baker Street number
☐ 220A
☐ 222C
☐ 221B.

490 The actor David Niven (1910 – 1983) was born in
☐ England
☐ Wales
☐ Scotland.

491 Florence Nightingale (1820 – 1910) was
☐ the founder of trained nursing as a profession for women
☐ a famous singer at the Metropolitan Opera
☐ an influential novelist.

492 The tough private detective in seven of Raymond Chandler's novels is
☐ Sam Spade
☐ Philip Marlowe
☐ Nick Charles.

493 Henry Purcell (1659 – 1695) was an English
☐ architect
☐ composer
☐ landscape gardener.

The Glenfinnan Viaduct is a railway viaduct in the West Highlands, Scotland.

494
Thomas Hughes' novel *Tom Brown's Schooldays* (1857) is about a young boy growing up at
☐ Eton College
☐ Rugby School
☐ Harrow.

495
Balmoral Castle in Scotland was built for
☐ Queen Anne
☐ Queen Victoria
☐ King George III.

496
Harvey's is a British company selling various types of sherry and is based in
☐ Newport
☐ Cardiff
☐ Bristol.

497
Martha's Vineyard is
☐ east of Nantucket Island
☐ in Cape Cod Bay
☐ south of Cape Cod.

498
'Defender of the Faith' (Fidei Defensor) is a title given to
☐ the Archbishop of Canterbury
☐ the Archbishop of Westminster
☐ the king or queen of England.

499 Which state has the largest land area?
- ☐ New Jersey
- ☐ Colorado
- ☐ Missouri

500 Which of the following BBC radio stations broadcasts mainly classical music?
- ☐ Radio 2
- ☐ Radio 3
- ☐ Radio 4

501
- ☐ Harlem
- ☐ the Bronx
- ☐ Staten Island

is not one of the five boroughs of New York City.

502 The well-known novel *Tom Jones* (1749) was written by
- ☐ Henry Fielding
- ☐ Laurence Sterne
- ☐ Samuel Richardson.

503 The Barber Institute of Fine Arts is in
- ☐ Boston
- ☐ Birmingham (GB)
- ☐ Baltimore.

504 Geoffrey de Havilland (1882 – 1965) was a British
- ☐ architect
- ☐ aircraft designer
- ☐ painter and sculptor.

505 The novel *The Scarlet Letter* (1850) was written by
- ☐ James Fenimore Cooper
- ☐ Washington Irving
- ☐ Nathaniel Hawthorne.

506 Which is an eye disorder?
- ☐ ophthalmoscope
- ☐ ophthalmoplegia
- ☐ ophthalmology

507 In the Olympic Games of 1936 US track-and-field athlete Jesse Owens (1913 – 1980) won
- ☐ five
- ☐ three
- ☐ four

gold medals.

508 US actor Lee Marvin (1924 – 1987) won an Oscar for his role in
- ☐ *The Dirty Dozen* (1967)
- ☐ *Cat Ballou* (1965)
- ☐ *Paint Your Wagon* (1969).

509 The ship owned by the organization Greenpeace is called
- ☐ Rainbow Warrior
- ☐ Green Guardian
- ☐ Rainbow Knight.

510 A name for a US soldier in the Second World War was
- ☐ trooper
- ☐ Tommy
- ☐ GI.

511 Sir John Barbirolli (1899 – 1970) was an English
- ☐ architect
- ☐ public prosecutor
- ☐ conductor.

512 Derwentwater is a beautiful lake in
- ☐ the Lowlands of Scotland
- ☐ Devon
- ☐ the Lake District.

513 Headingley is an area of Leeds and a sports ground where teams play
- ☐ rugby
- ☐ football
- ☐ cricket and rugby.

514 Who was not one of the famous Marx Brothers?
- ☐ Chatto
- ☐ Harpo
- ☐ Groucho

515 Who was not a soldier and a sailor?
- ☐ Sir Francis Drake
- ☐ Sir Walter Raleigh
- ☐ Sir Philip Sidney

516 The building of the Tower of London was begun by
- ☐ King Henry III
- ☐ William the Conqueror
- ☐ King Henry II.

517 The British title 'baronet' is not abbreviated
- ☐ Bt
- ☐ Bart
- ☐ Bar.

518 The novel *The Pickwick Papers* (1837) was written by
- ☐ Thomas Hardy
- ☐ Charles Dickens
- ☐ George Eliot.

519 US writer Ernest Hemingway (1899 – 1961) ended his life by
- ☐ causing a fatal car crash.
- ☐ taking poison.
- ☐ shooting himself.

520 The Royal Academy of Music, Madame Tussaud's and the Wigmore Hall in London are all in
- ☐ St John's Wood
- ☐ Marylebone
- ☐ Bloomsbury.

Fence decorations in Saltaire, UK.

521 What is a lacuna?
- ☐ a place where s.th. is missing in a piece of writing
- ☐ a rare piece of music from Indonesia
- ☐ a small lagoon on the coastline of Western Australia

522 Before he became conductor of the Berlin Philharmonic Sir Simon Rattle had conducted the
- ☐ London Symphony Orchestra
- ☐ BBC Symphony Orchestra
- ☐ City of Birmingham Symphony Orchestra

for 18 years.

523 Which airline went out of business in 1991?
- ☐ Pan American
- ☐ American Airlines
- ☐ Delta Airlines

524 Which statement about the Battle of Trafalgar is wrong?
- ☐ It was fought on the southwestern coast of Spain.
- ☐ Admiral Nelson died on his ship, HMS Victory.
- ☐ It took place in 1800.

525 The play *Peter Pan* (1904) was written by
- ☐ John Masefield
- ☐ Sir James Matthew Barrie
- ☐ Sir Arthur Wing Pinero.

526

The motto of the English kings and queens since the 14th century has been
- ☐ 'Dieu et mon droit'
- ☐ 'Honi soit qui mal y pense'
- ☐ 'Ich dien'.

527

When Jimi Hendrix, Afro-American pop singer, song writer and guitarist, died in 1970 he was
- ☐ 35
- ☐ 28
- ☐ 41.

528

The gigantic sequoias grow mainly in
- ☐ California
- ☐ Montana
- ☐ North Dakota.

529

The film song 'Chim-Chim-Cheree' is from
- ☐ *The Wizard of Oz* (1939)
- ☐ *The Sound of Music* (1965)
- ☐ *Mary Poppins* (1964).

530

The phrase 'town and gown' alludes to the differences between
- ☐ townspeople and students in the same town
- ☐ rich and poor people
- ☐ people wearing casual or elegant clothes.

531

Beacon Hill is an old and fashionable area of
- ☐ Boston
- ☐ Baltimore
- ☐ Philadelphia.

532

The tough San Francisco police detective in the US film *Dirty Harry* (1971) was played by
- ☐ Clint Eastwood
- ☐ Gene Hackman
- ☐ Lee Marvin.

533 Henry V was king of England between
- [ ] 1399 and 1413
- [ ] 1413 and 1422
- [ ] 1327 and 1377.

534 In the 20th century William Masters and Virginia Johnson became known for their study of
- [ ] heart diseases
- [ ] human sexual behaviour
- [ ] lung cancer.

535 Regent Street in central London joins
- [ ] Oxford Circus to Selfridges
- [ ] Oxford Circus to Piccadilly Circus
- [ ] Piccadilly Circus to Leicester Square.

536 George Macaulay Trevelyan (1876 – 1962) was an English
- [ ] biochemist
- [ ] painter
- [ ] historian.

537 The Tudors ruled England between
- [ ] 1485 and 1603
- [ ] 1327 and 1603
- [ ] 1485 and 1660.

538 Which is the oldest public school in England?
- [ ] Rugby School
- [ ] Eton College
- [ ] Charterhouse School

539 When did the Beatles separate?
- [ ] 1975
- [ ] 1970
- [ ] 1965

540 Disney World is a famous US amusement park near
- [ ] Paris
- [ ] Orlando
- [ ] Los Angeles.

541 Henley is a town on the River
- ☐ Eden
- ☐ Dee
- ☐ Thames.

542 Louis Burt Mayer (1885 – 1957) was one of the people who established the US film company
- ☐ United Artists
- ☐ MGM
- ☐ Paramount Pictures.

543
- ☐ The Conservative Party (the Tories) in Britain
- ☐ The Republican Party in the USA
- ☐ The Democratic Party in the USA

is sometimes called Grand Old Party.

544 The novel *The Life and Opinions of Tristram Shandy* (1759 – 1767) was written by
- ☐ Laurence Sterne
- ☐ Henry Fielding
- ☐ Samuel Richardson.

545 Aubrey Beardsley (1872 – 1898) was a well-known English
- ☐ book illustrator
- ☐ singer
- ☐ dancer.

546 The Domesday Book (1086) was
- ☐ a collection of prophecies in the Middle Ages
- ☐ a written record of the ownership and value of land in England
- ☐ an archive of obituaries referring to members of the nobility.

547 The British actress Audrey Hepburn (1929 – 1993) was born in
- ☐ the USA
- ☐ England
- ☐ Belgium.

A baseball game in Fenway Park, Boston.

548 In the USA in the 1950s McCarthyism was in extreme opposition to
- ☐ trade unionism
- ☐ Communism
- ☐ abortion.

549 Which is the smallest US state?
- ☐ Delaware
- ☐ Rhode Island
- ☐ Hawaii

550 Trooping the Colour is a parade in London
- ☐ to celebrate the queen's official birthday.
- ☐ to commemorate the British soldiers who lost their lives in the two world wars.
- ☐ to publicly present the latest army weapons.

551 Alan M. Turing (1912 – 1954) was an English
- ☐ mathematician and logician
- ☐ architect
- ☐ playwright.

552 In October 1555 Bishop Nicolas Ridley and Bishop Hugh Latimer
- ☐ published a book on the Reformation in England.
- ☐ were burned at the stake in Oxford.
- ☐ were knighted by Queen Mary I.

553

Sir Thomas Beecham (1879 – 1961) was an English
☐ conductor
☐ composer
☐ cellist.

554

Dorset is a county in
☐ eastern
☐ south-western
☐ south-eastern
England.

555

Robert McNamara (1916 – 2009) was US Secretary
of Defense under Presidents
☐ John F. Kennedy and Lyndon B. Johnson
☐ Richard M. Nixon and Gerald R. Ford
☐ Dwight D. Eisenhower and John F. Kennedy.

556

In 1987 nearly 200 people died on board the car
ferry Herald of Free Enterprise because
☐ the diesel engines had exploded.
☐ the doors had not been closed properly.
☐ there had been a crash with a tanker.

557

The Rio Grande forms the border between
☐ Mexico and Arizona
☐ Arizona and New Mexico
☐ Mexico and Texas.

558

Sugar Ray Robinson (1920 – 1989) was a professional US
☐ boxer
☐ baseball player
☐ golfer.

559

John Augustus Roebling (1806 – 1869, born in
Prussia) and his son Washington Augustus Roebling
(1837 – 1926) designed and built
☐ Manhattan Bridge
☐ Brooklyn Bridge
☐ Williamsburg Bridge
in New York City.

560 Chris Evert (b. 1954) was a US
☐ tennis player
☐ model
☐ swimmer.

561 Alexander Graham Bell (1847 – 1922) invented the
☐ refrigerator
☐ telephone
☐ vacuum cleaner.

562 The leading role in the US movie *Spartacus* (1960)
was played by
☐ Burt Lancaster
☐ Charlton Heston
☐ Kirk Douglas.

563 The wealth of the Rockefeller dynasty was originally
based on
☐ banking
☐ oil
☐ steel.

564 Before she began writing the extremely popular
Harry Potter series, Joanne Kathleen Rowling (b.
1965) worked as a
☐ journalist
☐ teacher
☐ librarian.

565 *Principia Mathematica* (1910 – 1913) was written by
☐ Charles Taze Russell
☐ Henry Norris Russell
☐ Bertrand Russell.

566 The Heriot-Watt University is in
☐ Edinburgh
☐ Dundee
☐ Glasgow.

567 The highest decoration in Britain for members of
the armed forces for bravery in times of war is the
☐ George Cross (GC)
☐ Victoria Cross (VC)
☐ Medal of Honor (MH).

568 Rosencrantz and Guildenstern are two minor characters in Shakespeare's play
☐ *Richard II*
☐ *Hamlet*
☐ *As You Like It.*

569 The SF film *2001: A Space Odyssey* (1968) was
directed by
☐ George Lucas
☐ Ken Russell
☐ Stanley Kubrick.

570 A Beretta is
☐ an Italian motorbike
☐ a household appliance
☐ a US make of small gun.

571 Which statement is correct? Sir Alec Douglas-Home
(1903 – 1995) was
☐ Prime Minister two times
☐ a member of the House of Lords and, at other
times, of the House of Commons
☐ a member of the Labour Party.

572 The Hillsborough disaster, in which 96 people died
and hundreds were injured, happened at a football
ground in
☐ Derby
☐ Sheffield
☐ Nottingham.

573 In Shakespeare's *The Merchant of Venice* (1596) a
sum of money is borrowed from a character called
☐ Bassanio
☐ Antonio
☐ Shylock.

Steam train at Pickering Station on the way to Whitby.

The famous Rosetta Stone with its hieroglyphics was discovered in

574
- ☐ Syria
- ☐ Egypt
- ☐ Iran.

Which statement is wrong? In the Union Jack

575
- ☐ the St Patrick's Cross is diagonal
- ☐ the St Andrew's Cross is blue
- ☐ the St George's Cross is rectangular.

The musical *West Side Story* (1957) was composed by

576
- ☐ Andrew Lloyd Webber
- ☐ Leonard Bernstein
- ☐ Elmer Bernstein.

Which is not a military academy?

577
- ☐ Milford Haven
- ☐ Sandhurst
- ☐ West Point

Arthur Miller's play *The Crucible* (1953) is about

578
- ☐ the Salem witch trials
- ☐ the Korean War
- ☐ the Second World War.

579 Which professional football team does not have 'United' in its name?
□ Leeds
□ Derby
□ West Ham

580 Which statement is correct?
□ The novel *Dr Jekyll and Mr Hyde* (1886) has a happy ending.
□ Dr Jekyll pays Mr Hyde for behaving in an evil manner.
□ The novel was written by Robert Louis Stevenson.

581 Sir Henry Bessemer (1813 – 1898) was
□ one of the Directors of the British Museum
□ one of the political experts advising Queen Victoria
□ an engineer inventing a new way of making steel.

582 *Leviathan* (1651), a book about rulers and their subjects, was written by
□ Thomas Hobbes
□ Sir Thomas Browne
□ Izaak Walton.

583 The Royal Albert Hall in London is
□ east of the Royal College of Music
□ south of the Albert Memorial
□ west of the Natural History Museum.

584 The novel *Dracula* (1897) was written by
□ Samuel Butler
□ Bram Stoker
□ Thomas Hardy.

585 The Royal Crescent is a long curved street in
□ Bristol
□ Wells
□ Bath.

586 In which of the following films did actor Sir Peter Ustinov (1921 -2004) play a character of eminence in history?
- ☐ *Death on the Nile* (1977)
- ☐ *Spartacus* (1960)
- ☐ *Quo Vadis* (1951)

587 'The Big Issue' is a British magazine publishing articles on
- ☐ crime and its prevention
- ☐ homelessness and unemployment
- ☐ urban developments.

588 Which city has the largest population?
- ☐ Plymouth
- ☐ Cardiff
- ☐ Nottingham

589 Who was a famous dancer?
- ☐ Isadora Duncan
- ☐ Lauren Bacall
- ☐ Jacqueline du Pré

590 Who played the main roles in these three films: *All the President's Men* (1976), *Kramer vs Kramer* (1979) and *Rain Man* (1988)?
- ☐ Robert Redford
- ☐ Tom Cruise
- ☐ Dustin Hoffman

591 The children's books *Winnie-the-Pooh* (1926) and *The House at Pooh Corner* (1928) were written by
- ☐ Beatrix Potter
- ☐ Alan Alexander Milne
- ☐ Kenneth Grahame.

592 As regards its population, Glasgow is the
- ☐ sixth
- ☐ fifth
- ☐ fourth

biggest city in Britain.

593

The Festival of Britain was celebrated in
- ☐ 1953
- ☐ 1951
- ☐ 1955.

594

RLPO is
- ☐ a police station in Ramsgate
- ☐ an orchestra in Liverpool
- ☐ a maritime museum in Plymouth.

595

In the U2-incident in May 1960 a US spy plane was shot down over
- ☐ the USSR
- ☐ China
- ☐ North Korea.

596

Tourists find the Stone of Scone in
- ☐ Edinburgh Castle
- ☐ Westminster Abbey
- ☐ York Minster.

597

There are
- ☐ thirteen
- ☐ ten
- ☐ seven

cities with more than one million inhabitants in the USA.

598

Camp David, the special home, office and camp for the US President, was first called
- ☐ Shangri-La
- ☐ Mount Vernon
- ☐ Monticello.

599

David Wark Griffith's silent movie *The Birth of a Nation* (1915) is about
- ☐ the French Revolution (1789)
- ☐ the American Civil War (1861 – 1865)
- ☐ the War of Independence (1775 – 1783).

Nelson's Column on Trafalgar Square, London.

600 Who stated that 'genius is one per cent inspiration and 99 per cent perspiration'?
- ☐ Thomas Edison
- ☐ Henry Ford
- ☐ Albert Einstein

601 New Year's Eve is called 'Hogmanay' in
- ☐ Scotland
- ☐ Northern Ireland
- ☐ Wales.

602 The great poem *Paradise Lost* (1667) was written by
- ☐ John Bunyan
- ☐ John Milton
- ☐ John Dryden.

603 The Royal Shakespeare Theatre is in
- ☐ Newcastle
- ☐ London
- ☐ Stratford-upon-Avon.

604 The English pirate Edward Teach (died 1718) was known by the name
- ☐ Scarface
- ☐ Blackbeard
- ☐ Long John Silver.

605

Ralph Vaughan Williams (1872 – 1958) was an English
☐ composer
☐ poet
☐ novelist.

606

Which was General William Sherman's (1820 – 1891) middle name?
☐ Shenandoah
☐ Burro
☐ Tecumseh

607

Which is correct?
☐ Edward III, IV and V
☐ Edward VI, VII and VIII
☐ Edward I, II and III
followed each other as kings of England.

608

☐ Albrecht Altdorfer
☐ Hans Holbein the Younger
☐ Pieter Bruegel the Elder
painted King Henry VIII and his court.

609

Which statement is wrong?
☐ A Minuteman is a hero like Superman.
☐ A Minuteman is a US nuclear missile.
☐ A Minuteman was a fighter in the American war for independence.

610

The RUC is the police force of
☐ Scotland
☐ Northern Ireland
☐ Wales.

611

Lord Nelson's ship at the Battle of Trafalgar (1805) was the
☐ Freedom
☐ Victory
☐ Cutty Sark.

612

'Black pudding' is
☐ a dark sausage made from animal blood and fat
☐ a dessert with an amount of bitter chocolate
☐ a sweet dark cake.

613

Dwight D. Eisenhower's (1890 – 1969) popular name
as the 34th President of the United States was
☐ Mike
☐ Davy
☐ Ike.

614

Which spelling is not correct?
☐ Hollywood Bowl (Hollywood)
☐ Holloway prison (London)
☐ Hollyrood House (Edinburgh)

615

At the Battle of El Alamein in Egypt (1942) German
forces were defeated by troops commanded by
☐ Supreme Commander Dwight D. Eisenhower
☐ Field Marshal Sir Bernard L. Montgomery
☐ Air Marshal Sir Arthur Harris.

616

The airplane in which Charles A. Lindbergh made
the first nonstop solo flight from New York to Paris
in May 1927 was called
☐ Spirit of St Louis
☐ Spitfire
☐ Endeavor.

617

Sadler's Wells is
☐ a theatre in north-east London
☐ a brand of sparkling water
☐ a group of wells in Sussex.

618

The Vietnam Veterans Memorial in Washington,
D.C., has about
☐ 72,000
☐ 45,000
☐ 58,000
names on it.

619
The centre of the large industrial area called 'Black Country' is
☐ Blackburn
☐ Dudley
☐ Wrexham.

620
The play *The Cocktail Party* (1951) was written by
☐ John Osborne
☐ Christopher Fry
☐ Thomas Stearns Eliot.

621
Jacksonville is a big city in
☐ South Carolina
☐ Georgia
☐ Florida.

622
The Monument in central London was built to commemorate
☐ the Great Fire (1666)
☐ the Union of England and Scotland (1707)
☐ the Great Plague (1664 – 1665).

623
The Hoover Dam on the Colorado River is on the border of
☐ Utah and Colorado
☐ Texas and New Mexico
☐ Nevada and Arizona.

624
The religious centre of the Mormons is in
☐ Boise, Idaho
☐ Salt Lake City, Utah
☐ Green River, Wyoming.

625
In rank a viscount as a member of the British peerage is
☐ below an earl and above a baron
☐ below a marquess and above an earl
☐ above a marquess and below a duke.

Whitby Abbey.

626
Which pair of cities has roughly the same number
of inhabitants?
- ☐ Plymouth and Stoke
- ☐ Aberdeen and Oxford
- ☐ Leicester and Bradford

627
When the Gentleman Usher of the Black Rod
gives the message that 'The Queen commands the
presence of the honourable House' he means
- ☐ Downing Street No 10
- ☐ the House of Commons
- ☐ the House of Lords.

628
Bristol has about
- ☐ 500,000
- ☐ 300,000
- ☐ 400,000
inhabitants.

629
Which statement is wrong?
- ☐ The emblem of the Republic of Ireland is the
  shamrock.
- ☐ The emblem of Scotland is the thistle.
- ☐ The emblem of Wales is the red rose.

630
Albert Sidney Hornby (1898 – 1978), an English teacher and writer of books for foreign learners of English, is best known for the
- ☐ *Oxford Advanced Learner's Dictionary*
- ☐ *Longman Dictionary of Contemporary English*
- ☐ *Cambridge Encyclopedia of the English Language.*

631
In 1535 Thomas More, Lord Chancellor under King Henry VIII, was
- ☐ sentenced to life.
- ☐ executed.
- ☐ banned from England.

632
The Isle of Man is in the
- ☐ English Channel
- ☐ Irish Sea
- ☐ Bristol Channel.

633
The American film *Schindler's List* (1993) was directed by
- ☐ George Lucas
- ☐ Francis Ford Coppola
- ☐ Stephen Spielberg.

634
Houston (Texas) has a population of roughly
- ☐ 2,300,000
- ☐ 2,900,000
- ☐ 1,800,000.

635
In 1789 Fletcher Christian led a mutiny against William Bligh, the captain of a ship called HMS
- ☐ Bristol
- ☐ Bounty
- ☐ Belgravia.

636
An art museum in Liverpool is called the
- ☐ Wallace Collection
- ☐ Walker Art Gallery
- ☐ Merseyside Art Gallery.

637 James Joyce's *Ulysses* (1922) covers
☐ one week
☐ one month
☐ one day
in the lives of the three main characters.

638 The E-type was produced by Jaguar between
☐ 1961 and 1975
☐ 1955 and 1969
☐ 1968 and 1982.

639 The US performer Harry Houdini (1874 – 1926) was famous for
☐ escaping from chains or locked boxes.
☐ sword-swallowing.
☐ juggling with three or more objects.

640 In some detective stories, Professor Moriarty is the evil enemy of
☐ Hercule Poirot
☐ Sherlock Holmes
☐ Lord Peter Wimsey.

641 Which statement is wrong? Wall Street in Manhattan is
☐ south of Chinatown
☐ north of Battery Park
☐ east of Greenwich Village.

642 Which of the following novels was not written by Sir Walter Scott (1771 – 1832)?
☐ *King Solomon's Mines*
☐ *The Antiquary*
☐ *Ivanhoe*

643 Dame Kiri Te Kanawa (b. 1944)
☐ was New Zealand Ambassador to England.
☐ was Director of the Sydney Opera House.
☐ is a critically acclaimed opera singer.

644

Anne Boleyn (1507 – 1536) was the
☐ second
☐ fourth
☐ third
wife of King Henry VIII and mother of Queen Elizabeth I.

645

The aim of the British Fabian Society formed in 1884 was to
☐ improve the standard of secondary education.
☐ change Britain into a socialist society.
☐ support British museums and art galleries.

646

Edwin Hubble (1889 – 1953) was a US
☐ chemist
☐ astronomer
☐ biologist.

647

The Mousetrap by Agatha Christie has been running continuously in London since
☐ 1952
☐ 1960
☐ 1948.

648

When people call you a bit of a Scrooge you are a
☐ miser
☐ pessimist
☐ masochist.

649

The SF novel *The War of the Worlds* (1898) was written by
☐ Herbert George Wells
☐ Orson Welles
☐ David Ames Wells.

650

The Book of Kells (8th century, a copy of the four Gospels of the Bible) was made in
☐ England
☐ Wales
☐ Ireland.

The standing stones of Stonehenge, England.

651 The football ground of Glasgow Rangers is
☐ Celtic Park
☐ Hampden Park
☐ Ibrox Stadium.

652 *The Faerie Queene* (1590 – 1596), a long poem in praise of Queen Elizabeth I, was written by
☐ William Shakespeare
☐ Ben Jonson
☐ Edmund Spenser.

653 The National Portrait Gallery in London is immediately next to the
☐ British Museum
☐ National Gallery
☐ London Transport Museum.

654 The Wedgwood company is near
☐ Stafford
☐ Stoke-on-Trent
☐ Stockport.

655 In Shakespeare's *As You Like It* (1599) Jaques describes the
☐ seven
☐ nine
☐ five
ages of man.

656

A Brummie is a person living in or coming from
☐ Birmingham
☐ Bristol
☐ Bradford.

657

The mayflower is the official flower of
☐ Massachusetts
☐ Virginia
☐ Maryland.

658

Which is wrong? Fifth Avenue in Manhattan passes
the
☐ Metropolitan Opera House
☐ Metropolitan Museum of Art
☐ Flatiron Building.

659

'Ich dien' are the words appearing on the official
emblem of
☐ the British monarch
☐ the Prince of Wales
☐ the British Prime Minister.

660

In the Trail of Tears (1838f.) the
☐ Sioux
☐ Navajo
☐ Cherokee
had to move to what is now Oklahoma.

661

Which drama was not written by George Bernard
Shaw (1856 – 1950)?
☐ *Saint Joan*
☐ *The Playboy of the Western World*
☐ *Mrs Warren's Profession*

662

Since William the Conqueror every English king or
queen has been crowned in
☐ Westminster Abbey
☐ St Paul's Cathedral
☐ Westminster Cathedral.

663 The oldest college of Cambridge University is
☐ Trinity
☐ King's
☐ Peterhouse.

664 New York City's first skyscraper (1902) was the
☐ Chrysler Building
☐ Empire State Building
☐ Flatiron Building.

665 Inauguration Day in the USA is always on
☐ the 15th of February
☐ the 20th of January
☐ the 30th of November.

666 *The Dictionary of the English Language* (1755) was compiled by
☐ Dr Samuel Johnson
☐ Oliver Goldsmith
☐ David Hume.

667 When the Dutch settled in the area that is now called New York City they called it
☐ New Haarlem
☐ New Amsterdam
☐ New Utrecht.

668 Between 1611 and 1616 Shakespeare lived in
☐ London
☐ Stratford-upon-Avon
☐ Warwick.

669 The Whispering Gallery in London is in
☐ St Paul's Cathedral
☐ Westminster Abbey
☐ Buckingham Palace.

670

As regards its number of inhabitants, Glasgow in
Scotland is
☐ bigger than
☐ as big as
☐ smaller than
Charlotte in North Carolina.

671

☐ Boulogne-sur-mer
☐ Dieppe
☐ Calais
was an English town between 1347 and 1558.

672

Worcester is situated between
☐ Stoke-on-Trent and Chester
☐ Birmingham and Gloucester
☐ Coventry and Leicester.

673

The Victoria & Albert Museum, the Natural History
Museum and the Science Museum in London are in
the area called
☐ Kensington
☐ Westminster
☐ Mayfair.

674

The oldest professional football club in Britain is
☐ Notts County
☐ Sheffield United
☐ Coventry City.

675

The phrase 'the white man's burden' was first used
in a poem by
☐ Thomas Carlyle
☐ Sir Henry Rider Haggard
☐ Rudyard Kipling.

676

The Sheldonian Theatre is in
☐ Cambridge University
☐ Oxford University
☐ London University.

Waterloo Street in Birmingham, UK.

Which of the three sisters in Shakespeare's drama is honest and loyal to their father, King Lear?

677
- ☐ Goneril
- ☐ Regan
- ☐ Cordelia

The Old Bailey is

678
- ☐ the oldest theatre in London
- ☐ a famous old pub in Fleet Street
- ☐ the Central Criminal Court in London.

According to the Arthurian legend, King Arthur and the Knights of the Round Table lived in

679
- ☐ Camelot
- ☐ Tintagel
- ☐ Avalon.

The capital of Alaska is

680
- ☐ Fairbanks
- ☐ Anchorage
- ☐ Juneau.

681 The first US space station was
☐ Columbia
☐ Skylab
☐ Atlantis.

682 The Lake District in north-west England is in
☐ Cumbria
☐ Lancashire
☐ Northumberland.

683 In the very popular US film *The Wizard of Oz* (1939) the heroine, Dorothy, is not helped by the
☐ Unicorn
☐ Scarecrow
☐ Cowardly Lion.

684 The famous US geyser called Old Faithful is in
☐ Yosemite National Park
☐ Yellowstone National Park
☐ Great Smoky Mountains National Park.

685 William Caxton (1422 – 1491) was the man who
☐ translated the Bible into English.
☐ advised King Henry VI in legal matters.
☐ set up the first printing firm in Britain.

686 T.E. Lawrence's (1888 – 1935) report on his military campaign in the Middle East is entitled
☐ *Truth and the Desert*
☐ *Arabian Winds*
☐ *Seven Pillars of Wisdom.*

687 The Smithsonian Institution
☐ comprises several museums in Washington, D.C.
☐ is a science museum in New York City.
☐ deals with economic issues in the USA.

688 An Aga is
☐ a musical instrument
☐ a cooker made of solid iron
☐ a technical device used in chemistry.

689 The Royal Albert Hall in London is
☐ square
☐ round
☐ rectangular.

690 The Allegheny Mountains are in the
☐ north
☐ west
☐ east
of the USA.

691 Which statement is wrong? Benjamin Franklin (1706 – 1790)
☐ was the fourth US President.
☐ was an inventor.
☐ helped to write the Declaration of Independence.

692 Mount Palomar, which is the site of the Hale Observatory with its large telescope, is in
☐ Texas
☐ California
☐ Nevada.

693 The comic novel *Lucky Jim* (1954) was written by
☐ John Wain
☐ Kingsley Amis
☐ John Braine.

694 William Schwenk Gilbert (writer) and Arthur Sullivan (composer) produced a number of
☐ serious operas
☐ musicals
☐ comic operas.

695 ☐ Kent
☐ Devon
☐ Essex
is often called the 'Garden of England'.

696

The first stamp in the world (in 1840, with a picture of Queen Victoria on it) was the
- ☐ Penny Black
- ☐ Farthing Red
- ☐ Shilling Blue.

697

A pugilist is a/an
- ☐ dancer
- ☐ boxer
- ☐ artisan.

698

The aim of the NASA Apollo Program was to
- ☐ fly to Mars.
- ☐ erect a permanent space station.
- ☐ fly to the Moon.

699

Judy Garland (1922 – 1969) was the mother of
- ☐ Liza Minnelli
- ☐ Mia Farrow
- ☐ Judy Collins.

700

In 1919 Mary Pickford, Douglas Fairbanks, Charlie Chaplin and David Wark Griffith established the film company
- ☐ 20th Century Fox
- ☐ United Artists
- ☐ Paramount Pictures.

701

The grave of President John F. Kennedy is in
- ☐ Maryland
- ☐ Virginia
- ☐ Massachusetts.

702

Which of these English kings suffered from severe mental illness?
- ☐ George IV
- ☐ George III
- ☐ George II

St Paul's Cathedral in the City of London, England.

703 The detective story 'The Murders in the Rue Morgue' (1841) was written by
☐ James Fenimore Cooper
☐ Washington Irving
☐ Edgar Allan Poe.

704 The Spanish Armada was defeated by the English fleet in
☐ 1588
☐ 1598
☐ 1580.

705 Mel Gibson is a/an
☐ Canadian
☐ Australian
☐ American
actor.

706 The famous Gettysburg Address was delivered during the
☐ American Revolution (1775 – 1783)
☐ Civil War (1861 – 1865)
☐ Mexican War (1846 – 1848).

707 Birnam Wood is a setting in Shakespeare's play
☐ *Macbeth*
☐ *The Winter's Tale*
☐ *King Lear.*

708

On Presidents' Day in February the USA celebrates the birthday of
☐ George Washington and Abraham Lincoln
☐ George Washington and John F. Kennedy
☐ Abraham Lincoln and Harry S. Truman.

709

Princeton University is in
☐ New Jersey
☐ New York State
☐ Pennsylvania.

710

President Abraham Lincoln was assassinated in Washington in 1865 while he was
☐ listening to a speech in public.
☐ chairing a meeting.
☐ watching a play.

711

The Rock of Gibraltar is crowded with
☐ eagles
☐ goats
☐ apes.

712

The aim of the Oxford Movement in the 1830s and 1840s was
☐ to enhance the university examination standards in Britain.
☐ to introduce some Roman Catholic ceremonies into the Church of England.
☐ to improve primary and secondary education at British schools.

713

As to its number of inhabitants
☐ Bristol
☐ Leicester
☐ Aberdeen
is the biggest of the three.

714

The first steam engine used regularly on the Liverpool and Manchester Railway in the 1820s was called
☐ Rocket
☐ Devil
☐ Rapid.

715

Queen Mary I of England and Ireland (1516 -1558)
was called 'Bloody Mary' because
☐ she ordered hundreds of Protestants to be
burned to death.
☐ she had hundreds of Catholics killed.
☐ she ordered all contenders for the English throne
to be assassinated.

716

Boston, the capital of Massachusetts, is named after
the English town of Boston in
☐ Gloucestershire
☐ Suffolk
☐ Lincolnshire.

717

When Captain Cook reached Australia in 1770 he
landed in
☐ the Gulf of Carpentaria
☐ the Great Australian Bight
☐ Botany Bay.

718

In 1990
☐ Edinburgh
☐ Glasgow
☐ Dundee
was named 'European City of Culture'.

719

Which statement is not correct? The Globe theatre
in London
☐ had a roof over the stage.
☐ had four levels of seats.
☐ was built in 1599.

720

The musicals *The King and I* (1951) and *The Sound
of Music* (1959) were composed and written by
☐ Richard Rodgers and Oscar Hammerstein
☐ Andrew Lloyd Webber
☐ William S. Gilbert and Arthur Sullivan.

721

Which of the following novelists used the pseudonym
'Boz' as the author of some of his early work?
☐ Benjamin Disraeli
☐ Charles Dickens
☐ William Makepeace Thackeray

722

Cape Cod is part of
☐ Massachusetts
☐ Rhode Island
☐ New Hampshire.

723

Al Gore was elected Vice President of the USA
under President
☐ George W. Bush
☐ Bill Clinton
☐ George Bush.

724

The novel *Roots* (1976) by Alex Haley is about
☐ an African-American family of slaves
☐ the first English settlers in Massachusetts
☐ the exploration of the American west.

725

The Clifton Suspension Bridge is in
☐ Bristol
☐ Swansea
☐ Cardiff.

726

The name Clwyd (a county in north-east Wales)
rhymes with
☐ fluid
☐ bride
☐ cloud.

727

Edmond Halley (1656 – 1742) was an English
☐ actor
☐ astronomer and mathematician
☐ physician.

The Royal Albert Hall is famous for holding the Proms concerts every summer.

728
The oldest scientific organization in Britain (formed in 1660) is the
☐ Science Club
☐ Royal Society
☐ Royal Scientific Institution.

729
Which English king had the epithet 'Coeur de Lion'?
☐ Richard I
☐ Henry V
☐ Richard II

730
Harrods in London is along
☐ Cromwell Road
☐ Brompton Road
☐ Kensington Road.

731
The San Andreas Fault is a long break in the layers of rock in
☐ California
☐ Nevada
☐ Arizona.

732
In the US TV series *Columbo* (1971 – 1993) Los Angeles police detective Columbo's first name is
☐ never revealed
☐ Peter
☐ John.

733 Which statement about the physicist Prof. Stephen Hawking is wrong?
- ☐ He was born in 1942.
- ☐ He worked at Cambridge University.
- ☐ One of his books is entitled *A Brief History of Space* (1988).

734 San Diego is situated in
- ☐ Arizona
- ☐ New Mexico
- ☐ California.

735 Sean Connery (b. 1930) was born in
- ☐ England
- ☐ Wales
- ☐ Scotland.

736 The Astrodome is a huge sports stadium in
- ☐ Atlanta, Georgia
- ☐ Houston, Texas
- ☐ Denver, Colorado.

737 Which statement about the British novelist Joseph Conrad (1857 – 1924) is wrong?
- ☐ Russia is the setting in his long short story *The Heart of Darkness* (1902).
- ☐ Conrad was born in Poland.
- ☐ Before he became a novelist he went to sea for twenty years.

738 Who was Time Magazine's Man of the Year 1938?
- ☐ Franklin D. Roosevelt
- ☐ Neville Chamberlain
- ☐ Adolf Hitler

739 How many Rivers Avon are there in Britain?
- ☐ 3
- ☐ 2
- ☐ 4

740 The main character in Dorothy L. Sayers' (1893 – 1957) detective stories is
☐ Albert Campion
☐ John Appleby
☐ Lord Peter Wimsey.

741 Amelia Earhart (1898 – 1937) was a US
☐ pilot
☐ dancer
☐ suffragette.

742 The play *Death of a Salesman* (1949) was written by
☐ Edward Albee
☐ Tennessee Williams
☐ Arthur Miller.

743 Heathrow International Airport is situated
☐ south of Chertsey
☐ north of Uxbridge
☐ east of Windsor.

744 The Sears Tower – nowadays Willis Tower and the tallest building in the world from 1974 to 1996 – is in
☐ Chicago
☐ Los Angeles
☐ Houston.

745 Wyatt Earp (1848 – 1929) was
☐ a US law officer in Wichita and Dodge City
☐ a gangster in Tucson
☐ a medical man in Tombstone.

746 Who was king of England between 1485 and 1509?
☐ Richard III
☐ Edward V
☐ Henry VII

747
The poem 'Gather Ye Rosebuds While Ye May' was written by
☐ Abraham Cowley
☐ Robert Herrick
☐ Thomas Carew.

748
The Easter Rising (1916) took place in
☐ Belfast
☐ Londonderry
☐ Dublin.

749
During the Industrial Revolution Sheffield was famous for its production of
☐ steel
☐ chinaware
☐ furniture.

750
The American George Eastman (1854 – 1932) invented a special
☐ camera
☐ motorbike
☐ radio.

751
Which statement is wrong?
☐ India became independent of the British Empire in 1947.
☐ India divided into two countries, India and Pakistan.
☐ Mahatma Gandhi was assassinated in 1945.

752
Wallis Simpson (1896 – 1986) was
☐ an American woman who married Edward, Duke of Windsor
☐ an English novelist
☐ a Welsh painter.

753
☐ Jack Nicholson
☐ Tom Cruise
☐ Dennis Hopper
was not an actor in the US film *Easy Rider* (1969).

Brooklyn Bridge, New York City.

754

- ☐ Clark Gable
- ☐ Gregory Peck
- ☐ James Stewart

stars in the US film *It's a Wonderful Life* (1946).

755

Smith & Wesson is a company
- ☐ producing chinaware.
- ☐ making guns, knives and bicycles.
- ☐ publishing books and magazines.

756

Which statement about Queen Elizabeth I (1533 – 1603) is wrong?
- ☐ She was Anne Boleyn's daughter.
- ☐ She became Queen of England and Ireland in 1562.
- ☐ Her sister was Queen Mary I.

757

The capital of Jamaica is
- ☐ Kingston
- ☐ Port-au-Prince
- ☐ Ponce.

758

The Juilliard School of Music is a US college in
☐ Chicago
☐ New York City
☐ Philadelphia.

759

Speakers' Corner is in the
☐ north-east
☐ south-west
☐ north-west
corner of Hyde Park.

760

In the US cartoon *Spider-Man* the hero's real name is
☐ Clark Kent
☐ Peter Parker
☐ Chris Reeve.

761

Faneuil Hall, the Cradle of Liberty, is in
☐ Concord, New Hampshire
☐ Providence, Rhode Island
☐ Boston, Massachusetts.

762

'The Fighting Téméraire' (1838) is a famous painting by
☐ J.M.W. Turner
☐ J. Constable
☐ G. Cruickshank.

763

Which of James Joyce's novels is written in an experimental style?
☐ *Ulysses*
☐ *A Portrait of the Artist as a Young Man*
☐ *Finnegans Wake*

764

The 'F' in John F. Kennedy stands for
☐ Fitzpatrick
☐ Francis
☐ Fitzgerald.

765

The postal abbreviation of Vermont is
☐ VT
☐ VE
☐ VM.

766 The London church St Martin-in-the-Fields is opposite
☐ Waterloo Station
☐ the London Transport Museum
☐ the National Gallery.

767 The former Hollywood star Burt Lancaster (1913 – 1994) began his career as a
☐ swimmer
☐ boxer
☐ circus acrobat.

768 Stonehenge, Britain's most famous prehistoric monument, is near
☐ Farnborough
☐ Crawley
☐ Salisbury.

769 Harriet Beecher Stowe's (1811 – 1896) best-known novel is entitled
☐ *Uncle Ben's Cabin*
☐ *Uncle Tom's Cabin*
☐ *Uncle Sam's Hut.*

770 Dr Joseph Lister (1827 – 1912)
☐ revolutionized operating methods in surgery.
☐ improved research methods in biology.
☐ invented an artificial language for worldwide use.

771 The main roles in the films *Kramer versus Kramer* (1979), *Out of Africa* (1986) and *The Bridges of Madison County* (1995) were played by
☐ Glenn Close
☐ Meryl Streep
☐ Helen Mirren.

772 The novel *Lord Jim* (1900) was written by
☐ Joseph Conrad
☐ Henry James
☐ John Galsworthy.

773

The Supreme Court in Washington, D.C. has
- ☐ eight
- ☐ nine
- ☐ seven

judges, called justices.

774

Which of the three American cities has the most inhabitants?
- ☐ Memphis, Tennessee
- ☐ Columbus, Ohio
- ☐ San Antonio, Texas

775

Which statement is wrong? Harold Macmillan (1894 – 1986)
- ☐ was followed as PM by Harold Wilson.
- ☐ was Prime Minister from 1957 to 1963.
- ☐ was a British Conservative politician.

776

The children's book *Swallows and Amazons* (1930) was written by
- ☐ Beatrix Potter
- ☐ Enid Blyton
- ☐ Arthur Ransome.

777

The film music of *Breakfast at Tiffany's* (1961) and *Charade* (1963) was composed by
- ☐ Henry Mancini
- ☐ Leonard Bernstein
- ☐ André Previn.

778

Charles Dickens' novel *A Tale of Two Cities* (1859) is set in
- ☐ Liverpool and Manchester
- ☐ Birmingham and London
- ☐ London and Paris.

779

Marble Arch in London is at a corner of
- ☐ Regent's Park
- ☐ Hyde Park
- ☐ Kensington Gardens.

A lifeguard station on Miami Beach.

The quotation 'Now is the winter of our discontent/Made glorious summer ...' is taken from Shakespeare's
780
☐ *Henry V*
☐ *King John*
☐ *Richard III.*

The Marks & Spencer shops in Britain were started in
781
☐ the early 20th century
☐ the mid-19th century
☐ the late 19th century.

The Woodstock rock music festival was held in August 1969 near
782
☐ Memphis
☐ San Francisco
☐ New York City.

The Mayflower is the ship in which the Pilgrim Fathers sailed from Plymouth to what is now the USA in
783
☐ 1615
☐ 1608
☐ 1620.

The Yeomen Warders in London guard
784
☐ St Paul's Cathedral
☐ the Tower of London
☐ Buckingham Palace.

785 Who was a famous band leader and composer?
☐ Jonathan Miller
☐ Henry Miller
☐ Glenn Miller

786 British agents are sent to foreign countries by the
☐ MIA
☐ MI5
☐ MI6.

787 The Zion National Park is in
☐ Idaho
☐ North Dakota
☐ Utah.

788 'The Old Lady of Threadneedle Street' in London is
☐ a hotel
☐ a nickname for the Bank of England
☐ a church.

789 On its way to the north the Mississippi River does not pass
☐ Memphis
☐ St Louis
☐ Nashville.

790 Which is wrong? In the British army ranking
☐ a captain is below a major
☐ a brigadier is above a colonel
☐ a major-general is above a lieutenant-general.

791 The Old Vic theatre in London is near
☐ Waterloo Station
☐ Victoria Station
☐ Liverpool Street Station.

792 'Ally Pally' is a London nickname for
☐ Pall Mall
☐ Alexandra Palace
☐ Lambeth Palace.

793 The English writer Lewis Carroll (1832 – 1898) was also a
☐ biologist
☐ mathematician at Oxford University
☐ a painter.

794 Heart of Midlothian is a Scottish football club in
☐ Motherwell
☐ Edinburgh
☐ Dundee.

795 Lord Mountbatten (1900 – 1979)
☐ died peacefully in his bed.
☐ was assassinated by the Provisional IRA.
☐ had a fatal car accident.

796 Nelson's Column in London is
☐ 34m
☐ 54m
☐ 44m
high.

797 The china and earthenware industries around the Potteries are around
☐ Stafford
☐ Crewe
☐ Stoke-on-Trent.

798 How many gates does the Thames Barrier (east of London) consist of?
☐ eight
☐ twelve
☐ ten

799 Dean Acheson (1893 -1971) was a
☐ musician
☐ US diplomat
☐ poet.

800 The National Health Service was established in
  □ 1954
  □ 1948
  □ 1944.

Congratulations!

Solutions

□ A
□ B
□ C

001A 002B 003C 004B 005A 006C 007C 008B 009A 010B 011B 012A 013C
014C 015B 016A 017A 018C 019B 020C 021C 022A 023C 024B 025A 026A
027B 028C 029C 030A 031B 032B 033C 034A 035B 036B 037C 038A 039A
040B 041C 042A 043C 044A 045B 046B 047A 048A 049A 050C 051C 052C
053B 054B 055A 056A 057A 058A 059B 060C 061B 062A 063C 064C 065B
066A 067B 068B 069A 070C 071C 072B 073A 074A 075C 076B 077C 078C
079A 080C 081B 082A 083A 084B 085C 086C 087A 088B 089B 090C 091A
092B 093B 094C 095A 096A 097B 098C 099A 100B 101B 102B 103C 104A
105B 106B 107A 108A 109A 110C 111C 112B 113A 114A 115A 116C 117C
118B 119B 120A 121B 122A 123B 124A 125A 126A 127B 128B 129A 130B
131A 132A 133C 134C 135C 136B 137A 138C 139A 140C 141A 142C 143C
144A 145A 146C 147B 148C 149A 150A 151C 152A 153B 154C 155B 156B
157A 158B 159A 160B 161C 162A 163C 164C 165A 166C 167C 168C 169B
170A 171B 172A 173B 174C 175A 176C 177A 178C 179B 180C 181C 182C
183C 184B 185C 186C 187C 188B 189C 190C 191A 192B 193B 194B 195B
196C 197C 198C 199B 200B 201A 202A 203B 204B 205C 206B 207C 208B
209A 210C 211C 212C 213C 214A 215C 216B 217C 218B 219C 220B 221A
222C 223A 224C 225B 226A 227B 228A 229C 230A 231A 232A 233B 234B
235B 236C 237A 238B 239B 240B 241C 242B 243B 244A 245A 246B 247C
248B 249B 250A 251A 252B 253A 254B 255A 256B 257C 258A 259B 260A
261B 262C 263B 264B 265C 266A 267B 268B 269C 270C 271B 272B 273C
274B 275B 276B 277A 278A 279B 280C 281C 282A 283B 284B 285C 286C
287B 288B 289A 290C 291B 292C 293B 294B 295A 296B 297B 298A 299B
300A 301A 302B 303C 304B 305A 306C 307C 308B 309A 310B 311B 312A
313C 314C 315B 316A 317A 318C 319B 320C 321C 322A 323C 324B 325A
326A 327B 328C 329C 330A 331B 332B 333C 334A 335B 336B 337C 338A
339A 340B 341C 342A 343C 344A 345B 346B 347A 348A 349A 350C 351C
352C 353B 354B 355A 356A 357A 358A 359B 360C 361B 362A 363C 364C
365B 366A 367B 368B 369A 370C 371C 372B 373A 374A 375C 376B 377C
378C 379A 380C 381B 382A 383A 384B 385C 386C 387A 388B 389B 390C
391A 392B 393B 394C 395A 396A 397B 398C 399A 400B 401B 402B 403C
404A 405B 406B 407A 408A 409A 410C 411C 412B 413A 414A 415A 416C
417C 418B 419B 420A 421B 422A 423B 424A 425A 426A 427B 428B 429A
430B 431A 432A 433C 434C 435C 436B 437A 438C 439A 440C 441A 442C
443C 444A 445A 446C 447B 448C 449A 450A 451C 452A 453B 454C 455B
456B 457A 458B 459A 460B 461C 462A 463C 464C 465A 466C 467C 468C

469B 470A 471B 472A 473B 474C 475A 476C 477A 478C 479B 480C 481C
482C 483C 484B 485C 486C 487C 488B 489C 490C 491A 492B 493B 494B
495B 496C 497C 498C 499B 500B 501A 502A 503B 504B 505C 506B 507C
508B 509A 510C 511C 512C 513C 514A 515C 516B 517C 518B 519C 520B
521A 522C 523A 524C 525B 526A 527B 528A 529C 530A 531A 532A 533B
534B 535B 536C 537A 538B 539B 540B 541C 542B 543B 544A 545A 546B
547C 548B 549B 550A 551A 552B 553A 554B 555A 556B 557C 558A 559B
560A 561B 562C 563B 564B 565C 566A 567B 568B 569C 570C 571B 572B
573C 574B 575B 576B 577A 578A 579B 580C 581C 582A 583B 584B 585C
586C 587B 588B 589A 590C 591B 592C 593B 594B 595A 596B 597B 598A
599B 600A 601A 602B 603C 604B 605A 606C 607C 608B 609A 610B 611B
612A 613C 614C 615B 616A 617A 618C 619B 620C 621C 622A 623C 624B
625A 626A 627B 628C 629C 630A 631B 632B 633C 634A 635B 636B 637C
638A 639A 640B 641C 642A 643C 644A 645B 646B 647A 648A 649A 650C
651C 652C 653B 654B 655A 656A 657A 658A 659B 660C 661B 662A 663C
664C 665B 666A 667B 668B 669A 670C 671C 672B 673A 674A 675C 676B
677C 678C 679A 680C 681B 682A 683A 684B 685C 686C 687A 688B 689B
690C 691A 692B 693B 694C 695A 696A 697B 698C 699A 700B 701B 702B
703C 704A 705B 706B 707A 708A 709A 710C 711C 712B 713A 714A 715A
716C 717C 718B 719B 720A 721B 722A 723B 724A 725A 726A 727B 728B
729A 730B 731A 732A 733C 734C 735C 736B 737A 738C 739A 740C 741A
742C 743C 744A 745A 746C 747B 748C 749A 750A 751C 752A 753B 754C
755B 756B 757A 758B 759A 760B 761C 762A 763C 764C 765A 766C 767C
768C 769B 770A 771B 772A 773B 774C 775A 776C 777A 778C 779B 780C
781C 782C 783C 784B 785C 786C 787C 788B 789C 790C 791A 792B 793B
794B 795B 796C 797C 798C 799B 800B